MARY BETH GILLILAND, M.ED.

SPECIAL EDUCATION
savvy

THE **MOM'S GUIDE** TO MINDSET
AND EFFECTIVE ADVOCACY
THROUGHOUT THE **IEP JOURNEY**

Author's Notes

I want to acknowledge all of the fathers and the special education journeys that they are on as well. It is definitely not my intent to overlook or diminish their role by focusing on the mom experience within the pages that follow. I realize that modern dads are more hands-on with all aspects of parenting than ever before, which is wonderful!

However, it's my deep desire to connect with and empower other mothers by talking to them directly, mom to mom. It's my mission to guide them every step of the way, as someone who has walked a similar path. Therefore, I'm sharing not only my professional experiences as a teacher and an advocate, but also, my personal perspective as a mom navigating through the world of special education with her kiddos.

* * *

Names and other identifying details have been changed in order to maintain privacy and confidentiality.

* * *

The information provided in this book does not constitute legal advice. The content is based on the author's firsthand experiences as an educator, parent, and non-attorney advocate. Any recommendations are meant to be general best practices for the parents of children receiving special education to consider. If you'd like assistance with interpreting the law and applying it to your family's specific situation, please consult with an attorney who specializes in special education law.

For Kathy,
A remarkable mother and friend,
and a passionate advocate.
You are deeply missed.

TABLE OF CONTENTS

INTRODUCTION

The idea for this book came to me in a vision during a year of spiritual awakening.

Seriously.

The story is definitely a little woo-woo, but too good not to share. Grab a cup of tea or a glass of Pinot and settle in . . .

For many women, our early 40s are ripe with possibility. There is simultaneously a sense of urgency to seize the day and a sense of freedom from the timelines that have stifled us in the past. Before we knew any better. We take inventory of our life choices and our accomplishments and choose to either stay the course or take a brave leap into the unknown. This is the fork in the road that I found myself standing at in 2018.

At the time, I was majorly struggling with clarity around my life's purpose. I felt both uncomfortably stagnant and vibrating with energy at the same time. Talk about a tricky juxtaposition! I intuitively knew that I was meant to do more and be more, but I had no idea what that translated to in real life.

Before I get to the good stuff, let me provide you with some context. I graduated from Rutgers University in 2000 with a Master's Degree in Elementary Education (K-8) and Special Education (K-12). As an Army wife, I had the pleasure of teaching students across the country, literally from one border to the other, from a racially and socioeconomically diverse suburb of Washington, DC, to El Paso, a border town in the western Texas desert, to a military town in upstate New York smack dab in the middle of the snow belt. My teaching assignments were just as varied. I worked with students in both general education and special education, across multiple grade levels.

I spent the last five years of my career teaching eighth grade in a high-achieving public school district in New Jersey. I wore a few hats there too, as an in-class support teacher for all subjects, resource room teacher, and Language Arts teacher in general education. If I had to pick a carnival ride to serve as a metaphor for my teaching career, it would be the Scrambler. Just when I felt like I was starting to get my bearings, I'd be launched in a totally different direction at full speed, constantly innovating, honing my skills, and then starting over from scratch. Over and over again. Looking back on it though, it was not only a wild ride but also the ultimate learning experience.

When I became a mom in 2008, I pressed pause on my teaching career. I was now in charge of a classroom of one and I threw myself into my new role with gusto. Little did I know that my sweet and smiley little ball of energy would end up teaching me so much more than I could ever teach him. I don't care how many degrees you hold or how much of an expert you are at your craft, nothing quite prepares you for the moment when career and real life collide.

You'd think an advanced degree in Special Education would make me adept at navigating the maze of Early Intervention (what we call the Birth-3 program in New Jersey) and put me in the driver's seat when it came to advocating for an appropriate preschool placement. In reality, it was quite the opposite. I was a clueless, anxious, emotionally disheveled mess. I clashed with our school district team early and often and feared I was becoming "that parent." I was overwhelmed by all I didn't know. All I needed to learn. I mean, how could someone with my background have such little knowledge of concepts like sensory seeking behavior, social language development, and what a preschool individualized education program (IEP) looked like? Google and I became best friends. We met up late at night and spent hours together. There was So. Much. To. Learn.

Just when I thought life couldn't get any fuller, we added another precious baby boy to the mix. That's when things really started to get fun. If you define fun as chasing a highly active toddler around the train table while nursing a newborn with one hand, that is. Survival mode was in full effect.

My husband and I experienced ALL of the emotions, and boy did we struggle during that tumultuous season. Time and time again we heard how lucky our son was to have such knowledgeable, dedicated parents in his corner. From where I was sitting though, I felt like a total fraud. There was so much I *didn't* know. I hardly felt like an expert.

I became all too familiar with the difficult lows and dizzying highs of parenting a child with unique learning needs; the blanket of sadness, fear, and overwhelm that hovers like a dark cloud on most days, as well as the pure joy that comes with each tiny victory. Those dazzling slivers of sunshine breaking through were the moments we lived for.

I spent the next 10 years advocating for both of my boys as they made their way through elementary school. Over time, my confidence grew and I added more skills to my advocacy repertoire. Simultaneously, the boys really began to thrive. They caught up with their peers in almost all areas and I shed tears of gratitude almost daily. I built a relationship of trust and mutual respect with our district's Child Study team and worked with a few other moms to establish a successful special education parent group. Everything was in flow.

And then 2018 hit me like a ton of bricks.

The year started off in the most excruciatingly painful way as I stood by a dear friend's side as she succumbed to breast cancer. You see, Kathy was my person when it came to all things parenting and special education. We met at preschool drop-off when our firstborns were three, and were each other's support systems through every twist and turn of their developmental journeys. We shared a special sisterhood. The special education parent advisory committee (SEPAC) that we started together was our passion project. We were both so eager to make a positive difference in our community by educating other parents and working closely with the school staff. We made a great team.

Kathy's passing sent me into a tailspin. I found myself wrestling not only with deep grief, but something more. A shift was taking place. I became acutely aware that time is precious and life is short. Was I doing everything I was meant to do with mine?

It's not uncommon for seasons of grief to give birth to clarity. This is exactly what happened for me. After much soul-searching, I felt called to devote more of my time and energy to special education advocacy. I had been helping friends and family informally for years, but the time had come to embrace the role much more boldly. When I look back on it now, it all seems so obvious. Every single day of my life for the previous 20 years had been leading me in this direction and preparing me for this moment. My life's purpose. I was so grateful to finally have the peace of inner knowing. I'm certain that I had a guardian angel gently nudging me from above.

I started a part-time job as a family advocate with a nonprofit agency in South Jersey. I was utterly scared out of my mind but very eager to start helping families. In my version of a perfect world, the IDEA, the federal law governing special education, included a paragraph stating that each parent would be assigned a personal guide at their child's very first IEP meeting. Someone to help translate all the special education jargon, guide them lovingly along their family's unique journey and most importantly, coach them to become their child's best advocate. Cue a little girl in the back of the classroom waving her hand back and forth excitedly and shouting, "Pick me, pick me, pick me!!!" The job description had my name written all over it.

Which brings me to a grand ballroom in Philadelphia and how the book you're holding in your hands came to be. I was attending a women's retreat with my best friend. During one exercise, a self-development coach stood on stage and guided us through a meditation to set our intentions for the weekend. Mine was simple and it came to me right away . . . *Clarity*. Intuitively, I felt that my life was moving in the right direction, but my pragmatic brain was still swirling with questions. Should I return to teaching? Would I be able to balance work and life? Was I having a midlife crisis? Should I grab my passport and journey across the globe *Eat, Pray, Love* style? I mean, the possibilities were endless.

After a full day of meditation, reiki, journaling, and sound healing, the magic began. I was jolted awake the next morning at 5:00 a.m. by a flood of images. There was a book about special education advocacy with my name on the cover. To be more precise, a series of three books entitled The Modern Mama's Guide to Special Education. The ideas flowed freely and easily, with crystal clarity. It was surreal. I even had visions of the cover illustrations and created mockups on my phone before climbing out of bed. They were modern and pretty and fresh, and looked nothing like the other education or parenting books on the shelf at the bookstore. I felt certain that this book needed to be written and that I had been chosen to do the honors.

In retrospect, the seed idea for this book had been planted many, many years earlier. It first took root as I developed an affection for the hundreds of students with unique learning needs that sat in my classrooms. Each one was a puzzle that I wholeheartedly devoted myself to solving. The roots grew deeper each time I handed tissues to a worried parent across the IEP table. I remember wanting so badly to calm their fears and assure them that their babies were going to be just fine. A tiny sprout broke through the earth the first time I sat on the other side of the table. The first time I heard my own shaky voice asking for a box of tissues. It grew taller and faster and blossomed with each step I took along the special education journey with my boys. And finally, the idea came into full bloom during the transformative year of 2018.

As an author, my hope is that I will be able to offer guidance to so many more families than through private advocacy alone. That potential is what really excites me. I hear time and time again that parents feel intimidated by the IEP process. They feel awkward and outnumbered at meetings, clueless about where to begin learning about their rights. I've searched the bookshelves at Barnes and Noble and the listings on Amazon. There is a desperate need for parent resources that are easy to understand, with concrete strategies that can be implemented right away, with parent-friendly language, bite-size chapters and real-life examples that resonate. Alternatives to the dry, dusty books full of complex legalese. It's my hope that Special Education Savvy helps fill this void.

One thing I want to assure those of you who are reading this is that you're not alone. I've worn similar shoes and have walked similar paths. I've felt the fear of the future and the overwhelm of the present that perhaps you are trudging through right now. My goal is to empower you if you're brand-spanking-new to the world of special education, and to help you take your advocacy skills to the next level if you've been here a while. I'm passionate about both. Thank you so much for inviting me along on your journey.

Now that we know each other better, let's dive in!

PART 1

Savvy Advocacy Mindset

• • • • • • •

CHAPTER 1
Mom to Mom

Parenting is hard.

Like, way-harder-than-I-could-have-ever-envisioned hard. Growing up watching the Huxtables, the Keatons, and the Bradys, it looked fun. The producers definitely neglected to mention a thing or two, or twenty-five.

When my first child was a few weeks old and colicky, and I was majorly sleep-deprived and weepy, I remember calling my mother to tell her two things. First, "I'm sorry." For anything that I ever did that was jerky or selfish or rude during the first 31 years of my life. I was a good kid, but she never deserved to bear the brunt of even one mood swing or bad day. Secondly, "Thank you." Thank you for loving me unconditionally in spite of the aforementioned bratty behavior. Thank you for enduring the less than glamorous parts of the job—the exhaustion, the diaper blow-outs, the sore back and tired arms, and for the many, many, many sacrifices. I had absolutely no idea how grueling the gig really was.

Parenting a child with a disability is even harder. There, I said it.

I often refer to it as extreme parenting, or super-parenting. It's Olympic-level parenting really, only without all of the medals, applause, and matching uniforms. You have all of the responsibilities that come with parenting PLUS a whole lot more added in.

You think the toddler years are rough? They are. But try adding sensory processing difficulties and an expressive language delay to the mix and welcome to Meltdown City. Get comfortable. You're going to be staying a while.

You think surviving homework during the middle school years guarantees you a first-class ticket to sainthood? It does. But try completing a research project on the Battle of Bull Run with a child with ADHD and executive function difficulties. Bring your patience and a cocktail. You're going to need both.

You think getting your kiddos to school on time in the morning is stressful? It is. But try it with a child who uses a wheelchair. Or a child with autism who only got one hour of sleep because their nervous system was in overdrive. Or how about a child with anxiety on the Monday after winter break when she can't find her favorite sparkly sneakers? Olympic parenting is in full effect and you, my friend, are going for the gold.

Take pretty much any parenting scenario out there and add a disability into the mix. It's likely that things just got more challenging, more complicated. And I haven't even mentioned the emotional aspects of parenting yet.

Basically, your Mama Bear game is going to be really, really strong. Why? Because the strands of DNA in every cell of our bodies are programmed to protect our young. The urge to shield is natural. It's instinctive. In addition to the typical concerns about bumps, bruises, and breaks, mothers of children with unique learning needs have additional vulnerabilities to feed our anxiety.

At some point, you might find yourself agonizing over questions like: Will my child have friends? Will he ever learn to read? Will she be able to play a sport? Will she go to college? Will she get taken advantage of? Will he be able to live independently? Will he get teased or bullied? Heavy stuff. Don't be surprised if stress gets the best of you at times. You're only human. If you've ever worried to the point of sleepless nights, frequent migraines, premature grays, and a prescription for Zoloft, you're in very good company.

I'm not mentioning any of this to elicit pity or sympathy. Rather, I'm trying to paint a picture of a shared experience and reassure you that if any of the above resonates, you're not alone. I'm trying to shine light on the sometimes painful realities that many of us experience behind closed doors. I'm trying to encourage parents to extend each other a nod of understanding and encouragement when presented with the opportunity. And I'm trying to remind the moms in the special education trenches with their children to extend themselves a generous amount of grace and a few pats on the back every once in a while. I see you, and I think you're pretty darn fabulous.

And I'm definitely not trying to make parenting into a competition. Especially since the moms I know are candid about the fact that ALL momming is hard. No matter what the circumstances, we're all barely keeping our heads above water and simply trying to survive another day. The good news—moms are built to do hard things—like becoming an even stronger advocate, for instance.

You've Got This

I'm passionate about encouraging parents to step up to the advocacy plate. Not in an angry or confrontational way, but rather in a collaborative, educated, and empowered way. There has never been a better time than TODAY to get your mindset right and go all-in.

There is a reason why the IDEA includes parents as full and equal members of the IEP Team. Your role is important! As a mother, the value of your intuition, experience, and input cannot be understated.

YOU are the expert on your child. How she ticks. What she most struggles with. What her gifts are. What makes him the happiest and the most frustrated. What his love language is. How far he has come, and how he feels about himself and learning. You've been there since day one. Own your well-deserved place at that IEP table.

Maybe you are as happy as a clam with your child's educational program and progress. If so, bust out the bubbly and celebrate, Mama! There's absolutely no better feeling in the world. But if you've been wondering if there's even MORE that you and your child's team of educators can do, there probably is. You definitely don't want to leave any stone unturned when it comes to providing the right interventions for your child.

Your Maternal Gift

Let's talk more about that little voice in your head for a second, shall we? It's time to stop what you're doing and listen to her.

Your maternal instinct first came into play during your child's earliest years of development, when your gut was telling you that your child seemed different from their peers in some way. When that little voice in your head first told you to pay closer attention to the milestones your child was supposed to reach each month. The advice I give to mothers of young children is always the same: Reach out to your pediatrician, even when your husband/best friend/mom and every other well-intentioned person in your life tries to convince you that you're overreacting; that you're blowing things out of proportion. That you're just an overly anxious first-time mom. That little Johnny will sit up and walk and talk and respond to his name when he's ready.

While it's true that all children mature at their own rate, do not let anyone minimize your feelings or concerns. Be courageous enough to trust yourself first. Consult with professionals who can evaluate your child objectively. If your doctor is dismissive or brushes off your concerns with a smug grin, find a new one. This is your very first opportunity to advocate.

As your child grows, continue to make sure that you honor your inner mama voice. When you think your second-grader should be reading more fluently by now, especially since his bedroom is full of books and you've been reading together daily since birth, keep voicing your concerns. Even if his teachers prefer to take more of a wait-and-see approach, stay politely persistent. Time is of the essence when it comes to remediating learning disabilities like dyslexia. If your instinct is telling you that something is not quite right, listen to it. Advocate strongly for evaluation and intervention without delay.

Some disabilities that impact learning are more difficult to detect. It's likely that your mama radar will start beeping even before challenges manifest themselves in the classroom. For example, let's consider the incredibly bright but chronically disorganized and absent-minded fifth-grader who coasted through elementary school with minimal effort and decent grades. As his mom, you can see the increased demands of middle school looming up ahead. How in the world is this child going to keep his materials organized and remember to turn in his assignments on time? And if his locker looks anything like his bedroom, you might as well add "HAZMAT suit" to the school supply list.

Don't hesitate to start a dialogue with your child's teachers and pediatrician. It's quite probable that maturity will kick in and your child will rise to the occasion of middle school. But it's also possible that an underlying executive function disability or ADHD might be at play. I see this all the time. Children who are bright and well-behaved fly under the radar. They're not a squeaky wheel, so they don't receive the "oil" needed to achieve their full potential. Students like these are at risk of slipping right through the cracks of the public school system.

Trusting your intuition is an important soft skill in your advocacy repertoire that I don't want to gloss over. I encourage you to tune in regularly and then take a conservative approach when it comes to your child's development and academic performance. It's always better to err on the side of caution than to look back with regret that you didn't act sooner.

You've got this.

CHAPTER 2

Overcoming Barriers to Parent Advocacy

It's not easy finding your voice or footing in the IEP process. In fact, there will be many obstacles standing in your way. I want to expose and unpack them here in the hopes that you'll be better equipped to maneuver around them like a ninja. They'll threaten to sabotage you completely or at the very least, slow down your efforts, if you're caught off guard.

Throughout my career as a special education teacher and as a parent leader in my school district, I had the pleasure of meeting and working with many savvy advocates. These warrior mamas are an impressive group. They work tirelessly to make sure their children have every opportunity to shine as brightly as possible. They're not burdened by excuses or deterred by the opinions of others.

To be clear, the path they're walking on isn't always lined with daisies. Sometimes, they appear to carry the weight of the world on their shoulders. You can see it in their eyes, and the deep furrows etched between their brows. They come to the IEP table prepared, arms laden with extra-large binders, relevant research, and a healthy list of questions.

They are the voice for their child's needs and wear many hats. In addition to being Mom and their child's biggest cheerleader, most have assumed the roles of coach, teacher, therapist, and counselor along the way too. The savvy advocate is always looking for opportunities to support their child's growth. It becomes their mission and they pursue it doggedly. They are determined. They are resilient. They inspire me.

As a teacher, I appreciated these motivated, highly involved parents tremendously. With follow-through on the home front, my students were able to make gains they never would have been able to achieve through my efforts alone. A rock-solid partnership between home and school is a powerful thing. I appreciated and respected the tough questions at parent conferences and IEP meetings because they kept me on my toes. The accountability made me an even more effective teacher.

But more frequent than the savvy advocate, I've witnessed a surprising amount of complacency and a lack of parental involvement in the special education community. For example, as part of my district's SEPAC group, we organize workshops for parents several times a year. I often scratch my head wondering why attendance is so poor. We're offering solid, practical information for free. Further, it is a golden opportunity to build relationships with the teachers and administrators in attendance. So why in the world aren't more parents seizing it? Why are so many content to sit on the sidelines instead of getting in the game? Why aren't more parents fully leaning into their roles as advocates for their children?

I'm certainly not one to pass judgment, and I find mom-shaming of any type abhorrent. I realize that every family's circumstances are different, but I do have a few theories.

Barrier #1: You're way too busy and way too tired.

Simply put, the modern mom doesn't have the time or energy to add one more side dish to her overflowing plate. She's living through a season of chronic overwhelm and teetering on the brink of burnout.

Further, there is way too much pressure on her to be everything to everyone, to excel in all areas of life. Motherhood, marriage, career, friendship, wellness, you name it. It's an impossible expectation. We're Busy with a capital B, and don't have the energy to learn anything new, especially something as complex as the special education system.

The reality is that there are only so many hours in the day. We're too busy keeping our kids alive and our bills paid. Our weeknight evenings are spent rushing around, chauffeuring kids to activities, grabbing Chick-fil-A for dinner and sitting on the sidelines of soccer practice.

We don't have time to scour the internet for IEP advocacy strategies or attend parent workshops. We have more pressing to-dos that demand our attention, such as therapy sessions to schedule and daily behavior charts to manage. For children with the most complex levels of need, meeting their basic needs can be a full-time job in and of itself.

If by chance we are able to carve out some time we'd much rather escape, either by bingeing our favorite shows on Netflix or getting lost in the social media scroll. Self-care habits like meal prepping, sleeping, and enjoying a social life feel like major indulgences. Exercise for some of us consists of carrying an overstimulated toddler out of public places, or blocking a teenager's attempts at self-injury. As a result, parents of children who think and learn differently are depleted in every imaginable way.

For many of us, what happens at school is the least of our concerns. It's the only time we can exhale, knowing that our child is in competent and caring hands for seven straight hours. It's a precious window of time when we don't have to be "on." The temptation to let the pros handle the "school stuff" while we stay in our own lane is hard to resist. Sometimes, we grab it unapologetically and check out. Been there, done that!

Barrier #2: You don't like conflict.

I'm no expert in human psychology, but I know that there are many women out there who avoid conflict like the plague. I happen to be one of them. We would rather stay mum, sidestepping confrontation altogether, than risk a showdown. The mere thought of disagreeing with someone openly, face-to-face, is enough to make our anxiety soar, especially when it comes to a topic that isn't our area of expertise. If we feel less than confident about something, it makes perfect sense that we would shrink, retreat, and try to blend inconspicuously into the background.

When it comes to educational advocacy, conflict-avoiders might ponder: *Do I really need to get involved? I mean, why fix what isn't broken? Why rock the boat? I'm being assured that my child is doing well. The progress reports I receive three times a year always state that she is "progressing satisfactorily." And the nice team of experts that work with her know so much more than I do, right? I can simply show up at school once a year for the IEP meeting with a smile on my face and a box of Munchkins in my hands. Woohoo—my job here is done!*

Their side of the conversation at the IEP table might sound something like this: *"So you think this placement is best for next year? Okay, great! You want to add this service and take this one away? Sounds good to me. Do I have any questions about the evaluation? Nope. So they did great this year? Awesome! Sure, I'll sign everything right now. Thanks a bunch and have a great summer!"*

Sound familiar? Okay, okay. So my storytelling is a bit of an exaggeration, but you get the point. Many moms are quite content playing the yes game and not making waves. People pleasing comes naturally. We are eager to believe that everything at school is happening exactly as it should be. The end.

Barrier #3: You don't know what you don't know.

The majority of parents don't have a teaching background, let alone a degree in Special Education. So entering the world of IEPs and 504 plans feels like being dropped off in a foreign land without a map or translator. The jargon can make your head spin and the paperwork is intimidating. This fundamental lack of knowledge is a huge obstacle to overcome. But as the saying goes, ignorance is bliss. Or is it?

Parents don't know what they don't know. Moms and dads have no idea where to go to start learning or how to get more involved in the process. And through no fault of their own, they're totally in the dark when it comes to understanding their parental rights. Many don't realize they can disagree; that they can request an IEP meeting at any time throughout the school year. That they can request that the district pay for a private learning evaluation. That they can have all of their parental concerns written directly into the IEP. That things don't have to be done the way they've always been done. And most importantly, that they have what it takes to become their child's best advocate.

If any of these three barriers resonate with you, please keep reading. YOU are the ones I wrote this book for. In the chapters ahead, you will find the tools to conquer each obstacle so you can step into your role as an advocate for your child more confidently.

CHAPTER 3
The Stigma of Special Education

This is a big one.

Truth be told, my deep desire to change the conversation about special education was a huge motivation behind writing this book. This topic really belongs in chapter 3 as a barrier to advocacy, but it's so important that it deserves to stand on its own.

Barrier #4: You fear the stigma attached to special education.

Sadly, it wasn't that long ago that dingy classrooms in the basement or makeshift trailers in parking lots were the special education norm. Children with disabilities were educated separately from their peers, in less than optimal conditions. Students with the most severe needs were institutionalized. Thankfully, we've come a long way since then. The flawed belief that some children aren't entitled to a high-quality education is behind us, yet parents may still fear the remnants of stigma that linger.

I've seen firsthand the emotional layers that parents have to grapple with in order to become healthy, effective advocates for their children—the varying degrees of denial, sadness, anger, fear, and even disappointment. Some describe a mourning process that has to be worked through after receiving a difficult diagnosis or first learning that their child is eligible for special education services. There are some moms in the special education community, most of whom have progressed further along in their parenting journeys, who find this admission extremely offensive, even ableist. I respect that viewpoint. But at the same time, I find that it unfairly denounces the very real and often painful emotions that so many among us encounter. Shaming others does not sit well with me. So, moms, be gentle and patient with yourself. Each of you are on your own time-line and journey with all of this. Your experience is yours alone, and the rest of us don't get to judge. Whatever you're feeling is normal and it's okay. Keep going.

Labels

I often see emotions bubbling to the surface when I'm working with a family that is brand-new to special education. Many are conflicted about whether or not they feel comfortable "labeling" their child. According to federal law, a child must be given a special education classification in order to receive an individualized plan to address his or her needs. In other words, no "label" equals no specialized instruction for your struggling child. This is your choice as a parent. Just like it's your choice to allow your child to take an antibiotic when they are diagnosed with strep throat, get a filling when they have a cavity, or apply anti-itch cream to their poison ivy-covered legs. After a quick analysis of each situation, most often the benefits of treatment outweigh the costs. Especially since all of these things are bound to become even bigger problems over time without the proper attention.

Labels in education open doors to interventions. They don't define your child. At least, I don't let them define mine. I made the conscious decision not to let a diagnosis or learning profile be the cornerstone of their identities. Nope, these things are just one tiny brushstroke on a massive, spectacular canvas. My children's primary labels are their names, Kenny and Luke, who just so happen to have great senses of humor, kind hearts, and fun-loving spirits to go along with a long list of character traits, interests, struggles, and talents that make them one of a kind. Masterpieces in every way.

But let's take a second and consider the consequence of NOT labeling your child. If a student is struggling in school without appropriate support, they are likely to come up with their own descriptors that are far worse. Take "dumb," "slow," "bad," and "unlovable," for example. Phrases like, *"I'm stupid," "I'm not good enough,"* or *"I can't do anything right,"* could become a child's internal monologue and are much more damaging. On the contrary, I've found that a diagnosis is often met with a sigh of relief. They finally have an explanation for why they've been struggling in school or feeling different from their peers. It's like a weight has been lifted off their shoulders and they become so much more buoyant and optimistic. As a parent, don't be surprised if you experience the same comfort.

Invisibility

The truth is that many of us are afraid to identify as a parent of a child with a disability. We don't talk about it enough, even among our closest friends and family members. But I fear that by NOT talking about it, we're perpetuating outdated stereotypes and stigmas. We're attaching shame to something that doesn't deserve it, and inadvertently sending hurtful messages to the very children we're trying to protect.

The majority of children receiving special education services in our public schools have invisible disabilities. Since you can't see them from the outside, they're easier to hide if the student and parent choose to do so. These kiddos have neurologically based differences that affect their ability to access the general education curriculum as it's traditionally taught. Examples include auditory processing disorder, ADHD, autism spectrum disorder, depression, anxiety, sensory processing disorder, and specific learning disabilities like dyslexia. As author, speaker, and parent educator Debbie Reber describes it, children with diagnoses like these are simply "wired differently." By talking about your experiences more openly, sharing your struggles and victories on social media, or getting more involved in special education groups at school, you may worry about risking your family's privacy, which feels especially scary when there are the Joneses to keep up with and a filtered facade of perfection to portray on social media. *Wink-wink.*

The older and wiser I get, I've come to realize that every child has differences. Every. Single. One. So why are learning differences or developmental differences something to hide? Instead of quietly sweeping atypicalities under the rug, I think we would all be better served, kids included, by more transparency. Let's teach children that "normal" doesn't exist. Furthermore, it would be painfully boring if it did. We all have things that come easily to us, and things that are more difficult. Instead of constantly hiding our struggles, let's shine more light on the subject. The time has come to put a stop to all of the toxic secrecy and fear. Let's come together and work harder than ever before to learn from each other. As a community, let's cultivate more self-love, empathy, and old-fashioned kindness.

[Mary Beth steps down from soapbox.]

In my opinion, becoming more savvy as an advocate for your child means so much more than learning a few new things about the law and IEPs. I hope you'll join me as an ally in helping to change the larger conversations about special education. There is still much work to be done. If nothing else, I hope that you'll find yourself better equipped to fully embrace your family's unique journey.

CHAPTER 4
Knowledge Is Power

When you become actively involved in your child's education, you're likely to earn some unofficial "degrees" while you're at it. I remember feeling like a quasi-occupational therapist by the time my child turned three. I had amassed so much information by participating in home and outpatient sessions, and then talking the therapists' ears off afterwards. Not to mention the books I devoured and the articles that popped up on all of those late-night Google searches. I didn't particularly WANT to learn this stuff, but if I was going to be part of the team that actively supported my child, there wasn't another option.

It's really no different than my early years as a wide-eyed wrestling mom. My wrestling IQ (and collection of gray hairs and hoodies) increased steadily over time. After watching the team practices, spending full weekends at tournaments, and asking a ton of questions, eventually I felt less like an impostor and more like a pro. I even started being able to name the holds my boys used on each other while rolling around my family room like bear cubs.

Again, did I really want to learn this stuff? Nah! But I knew it was important to my family, so I dove in headfirst. Okay, so maybe my entrance into the wrestling pool wasn't exactly graceful. And maybe your introduction to the sea of special education will feel more like a belly flop than a swan dive, but who cares? No one is keeping score. What matters is that now you're swimming. Or as Brene Brown writes so eloquently in *Daring Greatly*, you've stepped into the arena. Welcome.

Become an Expert

Nothing can really prepare you for the moment you receive a diagnosis from a physician or educational professional. Even if you've suspected something for years, there's nothing quite like hearing the words out of an expert's mouth or seeing the name of a disability typed into a report with your child's name on it. It can quite literally take your breath away.

I work with the family of an extremely bright first-grader who first reached out when Stone started having discipline problems at school and on the bus. He was often disruptive in class and would hit and kick other children, seemingly unprovoked. There were already two official bullying complaints filed, both resulting in lunch detentions. At home, Stone's behavior was equally challenging. He was lying and stealing from family members, and homework was a complete nightmare. Mom and Dad were left scratching their heads. Why in the world was their child having such a hard time making good choices? I encouraged them to speak to their pediatrician and request a special education evaluation in school.

Several months later, Mom had paperwork in her hand listing ADHD and anxiety as diagnoses, along with the recommendation for accommodations at school via a 504 plan. My first question to her was, "How do you feel about all of this?" Even though April was searching for answers and knew her child needed more support behaviorally, I knew it was going to be a lot to process. She admitted that her first reaction was sadness. Mom was happy to have some answers, but full acceptance would take some time.

It didn't take April very long to switch gears though. She now had a sense of direction and common language with which to communicate with family members and teachers. April had a long road of learning ahead, but at least now she had a place to start. Instead of getting angry at Stone, she felt sympathy for the aspects of this behavior that were legitimately out of his control. Her whole parenting style shifted, including the way she disciplined and structured the home environment.

I'm going to give you the same advice I gave April: "I want you to become an expert on your child's disability." Today more than ever, the sheer amount of information at our fingertips is astonishing. It's never been easier to become an educated advocate for your child. I have one important caveat though. Keep reminding yourself that this is a marathon, not a sprint. You don't want to burn yourself out in the first mile when you have 25 more left to go! Pace yourself.

Ask lots of questions when you take your child to medical and therapy appointments. Do they have any books or resources that they highly recommend? Check them out from the library and read them, along with magazines, articles on the internet, and blog posts written by other parents. Join Facebook groups and begin learning from other moms. Search hashtags on Instagram and boards on Pinterest. Sign up for online webinars and listen to podcasts. Treat this learning process like a graduate school course and get your study game on. Grab yourself a binder, notebook, and some highlighters. Get comfortable. Lean in. There won't be a final exam, but if there were, I want you to be able to ace it.

I want you to practice explaining your child's learning profile to close friends, family members, or your reflection in the mirror, until you feel extremely comfortable with the concepts. Once you can teach something to someone else, you've truly mastered the information. When it comes to asserting your spot at the IEP table, there is nothing more powerful than an educated parent who can fully participate in the conversation. Your confidence level and posture will transform, along with how you're perceived by the rest of the IEP Team.

In the Appendix at the back of this book, I've compiled a list of my favorite resources, experts, and places on the internet to assist you on your learning journey. This list is far from exhaustive, but it's a solid place to start. Each will connect you to more resources and more opportunities to expand your knowledge.

But I have another secret to make life a heck of a lot easier and make YOU a heck of a lot happier. It's the magical solution for every single one of you reading this, no matter what disability your family is living with. It's one of the most important pieces of advice that I have for you in this entire book, and it's actually pretty simple. Ready? Keep reading!

Find Your Tribe

I am blessed with a loving support system of family and friends. But when it comes to the emotional support I crave when it concerns my children and their experiences at school, there is a select group of people I turn to first. These are other moms who have faced similar daily struggles, fears, and doubts, and understand what I'm going through better than anyone. If you haven't found your tribe in the special education community, I highly encourage you to do so. It's a total game-changer.

Once you connect with other moms raising children with learning differences, they will become your lifeline. You see, friends with neurotypical children won't be able to fully relate to the stories you share. They may even unintentionally say something that strikes a nerve. A good friend will listen and do their best to make you feel heard, but these unbalanced conversations can leave you feeling lonelier than ever.

Find your tribe. People who understand. Moms who have traveled the same road and can point out the rest stops with the cleanest bathrooms and shortest gas lines. Those who will stop when they see you broken down on the shoulder, and either help you fix your flat or wait with you until AAA arrives. Moms who will clap the most genuinely and enthusiastically when your family has a win. An incredible community where you can take off the armor, let go of the facade, and just be.

In my experience, your best bet is to connect with other parents right in your own backyard. In New Jersey, every school district is mandated to have a group for parents of children receiving special education that meets regularly and provides feedback. Two other preschool moms I met at morning drop-off and I helped form our district's first Special Education Parent Advisory Committee (SEPAC) when our babies were just three years old. We were totally green with inexperience, but very eager to get involved. For starters, we wanted to learn more about our district's philosophy and programming. We also wanted to get to know the administration and staff better. We believed in the power of a strong parent-school partnership and were willing to do whatever it took to start building that for our community.

Over the next few years, the group brought together a phenomenal group of moms with a diverse range of experiences. We supported each other through the ups, downs, and all-arounds of parenting a child with unique learning needs. We shared community resources, advocacy strategies, and bottles of wine and cheese boards after our monthly meetings. When one mom posed a question or raised a concern, others who had already crossed that bridge could jump in with what worked for them. It was a beautiful thing. In retrospect, I wasn't only seeking information and guidance from my peers, I was yearning for connection.

If your district doesn't already have something like this, see if you can create it. Reach out to your local PTO. See if they would be willing to have a subset of the group for parents of children with IEPs who want to network. Or contact other local districts that have a group and ask if you can participate in their meetings. Reach out to your child's case manager and ask if there are any other families who are also looking to connect. Of course, there is always confidentiality to consider, but if all parties are willing, the school will hopefully be more than happy to assist.

There are many other ways to start meeting other parents too. Keep your head up and your ears open on the sidelines at sports and in the waiting rooms of your child's activities and appointments. When my son was taking a social skills class, the agency hosted a parent support group at the same time. It was so incredibly helpful that I ended up looking forward to the sessions every single week. Fifteen or so of us gathered around a large table with soft drinks and a plate of cookies, and talked about everything. Nothing was off limits. Struggles we were having at school, frustrations with finding the right physicians to meet our family's needs, and stories that had us sharing both laughter and tears. There was never a shortage of topics to discuss or problems to solve. We walked away with not only extra resources, but also new members of our tribe, and a sense of comfort knowing that there were other families out there walking a similar path.

I also encourage you to learn about the most current, evidenced-based treatments for your child's disability, and the most highly regarded experts in your area that specialize in them. See if they offer any workshops, trainings, or support groups. Thanks to social media, you can now find and maintain your tribe online as well. Start by searching for disability-specific Facebook groups. If you can swing it, try attending national conferences, meet other families, and then stay connected virtually throughout the year. Don't just hide in the shadows; become an active participant in each of these communities. Get engaged. Plug in. Start forming real relationships.

My wish for you is that you are motivated to get involved; that you will be able to summon the energy to find your own tribe. That you will experience the same gifts of friendship, mentorship, and connection that have made such a difference for me. Not only will you benefit personally from this Special Education Sisterhood, but the good vibes are bound to trickle down to your kiddos as well.

You may be thinking, *I feel like I'm doing fine on my own at the moment. Is all of this effort really worth it?* My response is a resounding yes! An educated, fully supported, and well-connected parent has the building blocks needed to become one heck of an effective advocate.

PART 2

Special Education 101

• • • ● ● ● ● •

Now that you've learned about the psychological framework needed to become a powerful parent advocate and you have your tribe in place, let's start tippy-toeing toward the nitty-gritty. Don't worry, I'm not going to throw you into the deep end of the pool just yet. Your Intro to Special Education class is about to begin . . . pull up a chair!

Educating yourself about both your child's disability and the special education process is imperative. Think of it like two courses that you're taking simultaneously. Knowledge acquisition is going to take place very gradually, over time. There will be some periods of time when your child's needs change very rapidly, and others when things are status quo for a while and you can take a breather. Try not to get too frustrated or thrown off by the inconsistency and unpredictability of it all. Instead, expect it. Try to embrace it even. It's just the way this parenting thing goes.

With each aspect of your child's development that you master, there will be a brand-new landscape to navigate just around the corner. Just when you're in a groove with the revolving door of therapists coming and going through early intervention, *Boom*—you're thrust into the new world of your district's Preschool Disabilities program. A few years later, your child transitions from preschool to school-aged, and *Pow*—you're in uncharted territory once again. *Do they still qualify for an IEP? What type of kindergarten classroom will be best? Could/should I hold my child back for an extra year to give them more time to develop?* So many questions and so many decisions to make. Each one feels heavier than the last.

The transitions from preschool to grade school, grade school to middle school and high school, and then school-aged into adulthood all come with their unique sets of challenges. Puberty in and of itself is a tricky time for families, but it can be even trickier to navigate for students with disabilities. Medications will likely need to be tweaked as bodies change rapidly, children become more self-conscious about differences than ever before, and then hormones . . . well, let's just say that you're in for one wild ride. An upside down, super-looping roller coaster on steroids. Hold on tight!

The truth is, you're going to need to acquire new information and skill sets every step of the way. You're never going to have all of the answers, and you're going to make a bunch of mistakes. But with time and patience, you will increase your knowledge and expand your repertoire. You'll start to feel a heck of a lot more savvy in your advocacy skin.

One of the best starting points is your state's **Parent Training and Information Center (PTI).** There are over one hundred of them spread out across the United States offering valuable information to parents of children with disabilities. New Jersey's PTI is named SPAN (Statewide Parent Advocacy Network). They offer webinars, fact sheets, and a vast collection of helpful links and resources. They even staff a team of parents who are trained to offer support and answer basic advocacy questions for fellow parents. All of their offerings are free and the perfect place to start learning. The internet can quickly become a rabbit hole for overwhelmed parents looking for basic guidance. I suggest utilizing your PTI as a reliable first step and then dig deeper as needed from there.

CHAPTER 5
The Special Education Journey

I have good news and bad news. Let's get the bad out of the way first . . . the special education world is totally rigged against us parents. It's like an amateur soccer player going up against the US Women's National Team. The entire team. Not exactly an even match, right? The pros have all the right muscles in all the right places. They've been training for years. They know all of the fancy footwork. Meanwhile, you are a complete novice, lacing up your cleats for the very first time. This is not going to be pretty. The good news . . . YOU, yes YOU, can become skilled ENOUGH to feel confident taking the field.

Where do I even begin? You've probably visited websites or picked up books about special education before. Perhaps you've even attended workshops or online webinars, but the overwhelm of acronym and jargon-laden content has been enough to make your eyes glaze over. I know. I've been there. And the irony about that statement is . . . I have a Master's Degree in Special Education!

Special Education Law was my least favorite class in graduate school. I remember rushing to the class twice a week, after a long day spent student-teaching in a second-grade resource room. The professor rambled on and on about some law called the **Individuals with Disabilities Education Act (IDEA)**. It was a total snooze-fest. I would have much rather been learning strategies to help James sit still long enough to learn, and Anna to remember the sound that each letter makes. I wanted to dig into the good stuff, namely helping real kids facing real challenges. The last thing I wanted to do was listen to a lecture about laws and timelines. I have a strong hunch that the majority of parents feel the same way.

And yet, I know this knowledge is essential for anyone who wants to be fully educated about the special education process and empowered to get involved. My goal is to make it as palatable as possible; to boil it all down to the basics. To start from square one and make sure that your foundation is solid.

In a nutshell, all children in this incredible democracy that we live in are born with the right to a free and appropriate public education. **FAPE**, as it's commonly referred to, sounds pretty straightforward, right? States and school districts work very hard to develop standards that they expect children to meet at each grade level. The majority of children, when taught the prescribed curriculum by competent teachers and supported adequately at home, will make steady progress. They will learn the necessary skills to advance from grade to grade and be prepared for life post-graduation. But what happens when things don't go according to plan? What happens when a child has a disability that interferes with learning? That's where special education comes in.

The Automobile Analogy

In public schools across the US, you can think of the K-12 **GENERAL EDUCA- TION CURRICULUM** like an automobile. In kindergarten, each child is given a standard make and model, designed to transport them safely and efficiently along their school journey. For the majority of students, it does exactly that. The very same car will take them all the way to the finish line, dropping them off on their high school graduation stage with smiles all around.

Each CHILD is the driver behind the wheel of his or her own automobile. And each grade level represents a fraction of the overall journey: 1/13, to be exact. A new TEACHER pops into the passenger seat to ride shotgun every year. They are the student's primary navigators, the ones holding the map, directing them where to go, and offering continual guidance along the way. Teachers also coach about the car's many features and capabilities, as well as the rules of the road. In short, they are auto experts. They give their drivers the green light when it's safe to speed up on an open highway, and they make sure they are proceeding with caution when the route becomes more like a zigzag down Lombard Street.

And you, the involved PARENT, are one of the most important passengers along for the ride. You make sure your child shows up every day and is prepared to give their best effort. You're the encourager, the trusty companion. Since you've been a constant since your child first put their keys in the ignition, your input is extremely valuable. After all, you know your child and their blind spots better than anyone. But, if you're being mindful, you know not to interfere too much with what's going on in the front seat. Your eyes and ears are always open, but you know when to zip your lips. You realize that under most circumstances, acting like a backseat driver does more harm than good.

Some children drive on smoothly paved roads under ideal driving conditions. For them, their school experiences are fairly uncomplicated. They coast along on cruise control, making it all the way to the end of high school with relative ease. Learning flows freely and almost effortlessly. Don't be surprised to see these students go by with their windows rolled down and some feel-good tunes blasting from the radio.

For many other students, however, the opposite is true. They encounter obstacles along the way, slowing down progress and making the journey much more challenging. Most hurdles are minor; for instance, an occasional drizzle, a small construction zone, or a random squirrel darting across the road. But others are much more impactful . . . think road closures with complicated detours, bumper-to-bumper rush hour traffic, and blizzard-like conditions in Buffalo. A significant amount of effort is going to need to be exerted along routes like these.

Let me make one thing very clear. There is nothing "wrong" with the driver or the car in any of these scenarios. Let me repeat. There is nothing wrong with your child. He or she has simply been handed a much more challenging driving experience. More hurdles will pop up in their path, and they will have to navigate around them. The standard automobile isn't equipped to overcome all of them. It can't meet all of your child's needs.

These drivers need a more customized, individualized ride in order to make adequate progress in a given year. And this makes total sense, right? How in the world could education ever be a one-size-fits-all model? Humans are uniquely designed. Children don't wear the same shoe size or the same clothing size, so why would we expect them to fit the same "education size"?

You may be wondering what is responsible for all of this variability. The vastly different driving conditions? The school experiences that are like night and day? The answer is about as complex as it gets. Neurological, biological, and environmental factors are all at play. Learning disabilities, cognitive delays, ADHD, autism, language disorders, vision loss, and various medical conditions are just some of the roadblocks that can interfere with a child's ability to progress through the general education curriculum. Look no further than the IDEA for a list of the 13 classification categories that make a child eligible for special education.

Crafting Solutions

Thankfully, the list of strategies educators can use to help accommodate students is a long one. Classroom teachers make minor adjustments to their instructional methods all the time in order to meet children where they are and help them to achieve success. The fancy name for this concept is differentiation, but I like to refer to it simply as good teaching.

Response to Intervention (RTI) is a framework that makes the intervention process more formal. Classroom teachers identify students who are at-risk and give them a more targeted, intensive level of support. School districts tap into resources like teaching specialists and small group instruction to differentiate instruction even more than a classroom teacher can on their own. At each step or tier within RTI, data is collected, progress is monitored, and hopefully, a student is able to catch up to their grade-level peers. Sometimes though, a student requires specialized instruction and services in order to be successful. They need special education.

Going back to the automobile analogy, SPECIAL EDUCATION is any physical change made to the standard make and model that students are given on Day 1 of kindergarten. Modifications might include a larger car, a different style, brighter headlights, extra leg room, more advanced technology, wheels with thicker treads, or an engine with more horsepower. The point is that each car is carefully customized for the driver in order to allow them to navigate around the obstacles in their way. This is the meaning of the "I" in **IEP**. An **Individualized Education Program**.

Sometimes the teacher riding shotgun and the parent in the back aren't enough support for a particular driver. Additional passengers, with specialized tools and strategies, are needed to hop in the car and assist. Special education teachers, speech therapists, guidance counselors, and behaviorists are just some of the possible experts that might be called upon. These are individuals who can recommend shortcuts to avoid obstacles altogether. Or they may suggest more frequent oil changes, a different type of fuel, or a brand of high-tech wiper blades that the general education teacher is unaware of. With the right car and combination of passengers, the student will be better equipped to handle anything that comes his or her way. They will be cruising along in no time!

The Bigger Issue

I want to take a second to talk about special education beyond academics. For most students, learning differences have an impact on emotional well-being as well. Stop and think for a second about how you typically respond as a driver when confronted with challenges on the road. For instance, how do you feel when driving through a downpour and you can barely see the car in front of you? Or how about when there's a traffic accident ahead and the rubbernecking is going to make you late for parent pick-up? I know for me, I tend to grip the steering wheel more tightly and tense my neck and shoulders. I can feel my pulse and anxiety level rising. For some, stressful events can even lead to extreme frustration and anger. We've all heard the term *road rage*, right? If you're from the awesome state of New Jersey, like I am, you might even act out a bit by firing off some colorful language or hand gestures. No judgment here. Feeling helpless behind the wheel can trigger all types of responses.

For students who encounter obstacles along their educational highways, the emotions generated can be very similar. Learning becomes more stressful and a heck of a lot less enjoyable. Instead of glancing around to enjoy the view from time to time, struggling students are unable to take their eyes off the road. And if they do get a chance to sneak a peek, the sight of classmates whizzing by without a care in the world may make them feel even more defeated. *Why do others have roads that are clear and skies that are sunny? Why do I have so many potholes in my way? What if I get left behind? This isn't fair!* When thoughts like these start to swirl, emotions rise. Over time, a student's developing sense of self can take a major hit.

If not addressed properly, learning problems can morph into behavior problems. Acting out in class, defiance, becoming the class clown, and even aggression are some of the troubling responses I've seen when a child's academic needs aren't being met. Some children get pigeonholed as disruptive troublemakers when the root of the problem is really an underlying learning difficulty. Sadly, these students are frequent flyers to the principal's office. They are the recipients of detentions and suspensions. They receive an Emotional Disturbance classification when it's not warranted. The system is failing them.

I heard a statistic the other day that stopped me in my tracks. According to research gathered by The Literacy Project Foundation in 2017, up to 75 percent of the prison population cannot read. Further, 85 percent of juvenile offenders have trouble reading. It makes me wonder how many of them were once young children who struggled in school. And after years of repeated failure and frustration, they just stopped trying. They gave up. Perhaps this is what propelled them down a much darker path. I can't help but imagine how different their fate would have been if they'd received the appropriate interventions as a youngster.

It's one of the many reasons why I'm so passionate about making sure that special education is done right. The consequences of the alternative are far too great. Moms, your role in this effort is vital. There's a spot in your child's car with your name on it. Buckle up—let's do this!

CHAPTER 6

Evaluation and Eligibility

Let's start at the very beginning of the special education process. The information here will be particularly helpful for the moms who are brand-new to the journey. But, since a student's eligibility status is reviewed every three years, with the option to reevaluate at that time if not sooner, the information is relevant to all. I'm also going to highlight a few of the questions that I hear from parents most often.

The Evaluation Process

Q: What are some of the warning signs to indicate that a special education evaluation (or reevaluation) is warranted?

As a parent, you will likely be the first to notice when something is out of the norm for your child. Listen to your intuition. Some other signs include below-average report card grades, poor test scores, not meeting grade level benchmarks, school refusal, concerns raised by your child's teacher, and frequent reports that your child is misbehaving. Confusion, frustration and tears at homework time along with comments like, "This is too hard," "I hate school," and "I'm so dumb!" are also red flags.

The first thing you should do is reach out to your child's teacher to share your concerns. What does he or she observe in the classroom? Has anything grabbed their attention? Are there any strategies you can try at home? Consistent parent-teacher communication is going to be really important as you work together to get to the bottom of what is going on. In the meantime, you can get the evaluation ball rolling.

Step 1: Request an evaluation.

If you suspect that your child has a disability interfering with their ability to make educational progress, it's your parental right to request a special education evaluation. Send a simple email to your child's principal stating your request, along with a bulleted list of your concerns. It's also helpful to include any interventions that have already been tried up to that point (private tutoring, basic skills instruction, working with a teacher one-on-one or in small groups, etc.). If a teacher suspects the presence of a disability, they are obligated to initiate the evaluation process as well.

Step 2: Attend an Evaluation Planning Meeting.

Once the school receives your written evaluation request, they will invite you to an Evaluation Planning Meeting to discuss your concerns. Check your state regulations to see if a timeline applies. In New Jersey, the meeting must take place within 20 days. Together with your child's teachers and other staff members who are experts in child development and learning, you will decide if an evaluation is warranted. If it is, the team will identify the specific areas of performance to be assessed and develop a written plan.

Q: What tests will my child be given?

The most common components of a special education evaluation include the **Learning Evaluation,** which tests academic skills such as reading, written expression, and mathematics, and the **Psychological Evaluation,** which measures intelligence and overall cognitive functioning. Evaluators are looking for evidence that a disability exists. A significant enough discrepancy between a child's IQ (academic potential) and achievement (actual performance) is one of the ways to detect a specific learning disability. If a child has a medical diagnosis that is believed to be impacting their school performance, the IEP Team will also take that into account. A Social History is a narrative written after an in-depth interview with the parent and a review of the child's background information. This report is typically put together by a school social worker or guidance counselor.

Step 3: Advocate for evaluation in ALL areas of suspected disability.

The IDEA is very clear about the school district's responsibility to evaluate in ALL areas of suspected disability, per 20 USC § 1414 (b)(3)(B). It's important for parents to know that special education evaluations and services aren't JUST for academics. If you believe that your child is struggling in other domains, you can and should request a corresponding evaluation. Additional areas include, but are not limited to, speech, social skills, executive functioning (organization, planning, sustained attention), emotional regulation, behavior, motor skills, sensory processing, adaptive skills, mental health, and communication. Many of these are overlooked far too often, so it's important that parents speak up during the evaluation planning part of the IEP process. The goal is to get as clear a picture as possible of your child as a learner. The only way to do this is through an evaluation using standardized measures. If a school district doesn't already have a professional on staff who can evaluate a particular skill set, they aren't off the hook. They can bring in an expert to get the job done or pay for the assessment to be performed in the private setting.

Evaluations identify areas of need. Areas of need lead to IEP goals. And IEP goals dictate the services that your child will receive. So, if you want your child to receive specialized instruction in a particular skill area, make sure it gets formally evaluated.

Q: What if the school says they have to "wait and see" how my child responds to other interventions first?

Sometimes, a school district will suggest delaying a full special education evaluation until they see how a student responds to other, less intensive interventions first. I call this the "wait and see" approach. Unfortunately, it often becomes the "wait and fail" approach, which is totally unacceptable. But let me explain. The **Multi-Tier System of Supports (MTSS)** model that many schools follow is effective most of the time. I'm a fan! Struggling students are first identified by the classroom teacher and then given additional targeted instruction to help them get caught up to grade level standards. Children who aren't making sufficient progress in a timely manner will then move on to the next tier in the framework. The step-by-step system generally follows this sequence:

Tier 3 – Individualized support

Tier 2 – Small group intervention

Tier 1 – Whole-class strategies

Response to Intervention (RTI) is an example of MTSS that is widely embraced across the country. You may even hear the terms being used interchangeably.

BUT, listen carefully to your mama gut on this one! If your intuition is telling you that something more significant is going on, you should absolutely advocate for a full evaluation without delay. And the US Department of Education supports you! Their Office of Special Education Programs (OSEP) has specifically, and repeatedly, stated that RTI is NOT to be used to delay or deny a special education evaluation. The two can happen simultaneously. I've had numerous parents tell me that their child's teacher spoke to them off the record or strongly hinted that they were seeing signs of a disability. If a teacher is willing to stick their neck out for your family in this way, please pay attention. Time is of the essence. The earlier a child receives the intervention they need, the better the long-term outcome.

Step 4: Sign consent to evaluate.

According to federal law, the school cannot conduct an evaluation without your written permission. Once a parent provides consent, there is a strict timeline that must be followed. There is some variability from state to state, so definitely check your state regulations. The majority of the time, a school district has 60 calendar days to complete the evaluation process. New Jersey words it a little differently and abides by a 90-day timeline. During that time period, students must be evaluated and begin special education services with an appropriate IEP if they are deemed eligible.

Step 5: Read the evaluation reports carefully.

Actually take the time to read through each page of the reports that are mailed to you. Generally these things are lengthy and very technical, so it may even take several sittings. Grab some caffeine, a pen, and a highlighter. Jot down your questions in the margins as you go. Highlight the sections that identify your child's biggest problem areas. This is the information you're going to want to discuss more thoroughly and develop an action plan for at the next meeting.

Eligibility

Once evaluations have been completed, you will be invited to a meeting to go over the results and determine if your child is eligible for special education services. Please make sure that you request a copy of all evaluation reports prior to the meeting so you have ample time to review them. In New Jersey, parents must receive copies of the reports at least 10 days prior to a meeting. Like with so many things, the timeline varies from state to state. Double-check your state regulations to get clear about your rights.

The bottom line is this . . . if your meeting is in a few days and you haven't received all of the reports yet, definitely reach out to request them. Should you have to do this? No. But it's an imperfect world, and most Special Services teams are stretched extremely thin. Truth bomb time, moms! Knowing your rights, and asserting them when needed, is YOUR responsibility.

Step 6: Attend an Eligibility Determination Meeting.

We are going to take a deeper dive into the language of the law for a few minutes. It's important that you have a basic understanding of the decision-making process around eligibility, especially if you are at odds with your school district about whether or not your child qualifies for special education.

In order to qualify for an IEP under IDEA, there are very specific criteria that need to be met.

1) The student is a "child with a disability."

2) The disability adversely affects the student's educational performance.

3) As a result, the student requires special education and related services.

This is exactly what will be discussed at an eligibility meeting. If the rest of the team gathered concludes that your child does NOT qualify for special education, but you feel strongly that they do, you're going to need to understand the nuances of each in order to advocate effectively. Let's unpack them a bit further by turning each criterion into a question.

Question #1: *Is the student a "child with a disability"?*

In other words, does the student meet the criteria for one of these 13 educational disability classifications under federal and state law?

1) Autism

2) Deaf-blindness

3) Deafness

4) Emotional disturbance

5) Hearing impairment

6) Intellectual disability

7) Multiple disabilities

8) Orthopedic impairment

9) Other health impairment

10) Specific learning disability

11) Speech or language impairment

12) Traumatic brain injury

13) Visual impairment, including blindness

For a brief description of each, consult the IDEA or your state's regulations. It's important to note that these are NOT medical diagnoses. Rather, they are educational classifications. This is an important distinction, and one that is often confusing for parents. You may hear diagnoses received from a physician referred to as the "medical model," while a disability classification assigned by educators following the evaluation process is the "educational model." They are not synonymous. A medical diagnosis should be considered by the IEP Team and may be used as evidence to corroborate an educational disability classification. But a medical diagnosis does not automatically justify the need for special education.

Question #2: *Does the disability adversely affect the child's educational performance?*

This is a tricky one. Parents will often hear the argument that their child doesn't need special education because their "grades are okay," or "they're doing fine in school." This gets me fired up every single time! Why? First of all, grades are subjective measures of achievement. How the student is performing on standardized measures can be slightly more helpful; but still, numbers and letters don't always tell the whole story. Reread the language in criteria #2 again. It doesn't say "academic" performance, it says "educational." The meaning of *educational* is much broader than how a child is doing on their report card. It also takes into account a student's developmental and **functional performance**. How is the student functioning overall in their learning environment? This encompasses routine activities of everyday living such as walking through the hallways, maneuvering through the lunch line, eating, making friends, communicating with peers, and behavior across a variety of settings.

For example, I work with the parents of an eighth grade student on the autism spectrum. Charlie has a 140 IQ, straight As on his report card, and is one of the coolest kids I've ever had the pleasure of meeting. In spite of his cognitive abilities and strong academic record, Charlie has an IEP to address his difficulties with social skills, pragmatic language skills, and emotional regulation. Working cooperatively with peers, communicating with teachers, and coping with frustration appropriately are functional skills that a middle school student needs. Unfortunately, Charlie struggles in each area on a daily basis. He was frequently the cause of classroom disruptions, and even got suspended for fighting with other students in the hallway who were teasing him. With the help of a well-written IEP and the support of weekly sessions with the school psychologist, Charlie is now getting all of his needs met and having a great school year.

Question #3: *As a result of their disability, does the child require special education and related services?*

Special education is "**specially designed instruction**," which IDEA defines as ". . . adapting, as appropriate to the needs of an eligible child under this part, the *content, methodology,* or *delivery of instruction* . . . to address the unique needs of the child that result from the child's disability" (34 CFR § 300.39(b)(3)).

Changes to *content* refers to the knowledge and skills being taught. Does the child require an alternative curriculum or texts? Tests and quizzes that assess less content compared to peers? Instruction in basic life skills?

Changes to *methodology* means the instructional strategies or programs used. Does the child require Applied Behavior Analysis (ABA) in order to learn? Does the child need a structured literacy program to learn how to read? Does the child need an individualized behavior plan? Does the child need more multisensory techniques incorporated?

Changes to the *delivery of instruction* means the manner in which instruction is delivered. Does the child need a smaller group setting or 1:1 instruction? Does the child need the support of a special education co-teacher? Does the child need assistive technology in order to meet their needs?

To reiterate, a student must meet ALL three criteria (sometimes referred to as "prongs") in order to be eligible for special education. Disputes about eligibility are extremely common. Typically, parents are advocating for their kiddo to get more help but the school district insists that the child doesn't qualify for an IEP. If this is your situation, you may want to consider having your child evaluated privately. More comprehensive testing results, a diagnosis of some type, and/or recommendations from an expert in the field can be extremely persuasive. You'll learn more about how to request and obtain an **Independent Educational Evaluation (IEE)** in chapters 13 and 20. That might be the most helpful advocacy route to take, especially if your health insurance doesn't cover the assessments that are needed.

Step 7: Help create an Individualized Education Program.

When a child is determined eligible for special education, the next step is to create an action plan to meet their needs. If time allows, the parents and the other educators gathered may move immediately into the process of drafting an IEP. If not, another meeting will be scheduled for this purpose. Once a parent has been handed the keys to the special education kingdom, their job as an advocate moves into a new phase. From this point forward, the IEP takes center stage. You're going to want to get very familiar with all of its parts and the purpose of each. Being IEP savvy is so critical that I'm devoting an entire chapter to it.

504 Plans

Remember that just because your child has a medical diagnosis from a physician, it does NOT mean that he or she automatically meets the criteria for an "educational classification." For example, a child could receive a medical diagnosis of ADHD, but if it's not impacting their educational performance adversely enough to require specialized instruction, they would NOT be eligible for an IEP. A student like this would likely meet the criteria for **accommodations** under **Section 504 of the Rehabilitation Act of 1973** though. Like the Americans with Disabilities Act (ADA), Section 504 is a civil rights law that prohibits discrimination against individuals with disabilities.

If a child has a disability that affects a "major life activity," he or she can receive accommodations through a 504 plan. The purpose of a 504 plan is to remove any barriers that are preventing the student from accessing their education. It doesn't change WHAT a child is taught, but rather HOW the instruction is delivered.

For instance, if a child with ADHD has a hard time staying in their seat, a 504 plan might include frequent movement breaks and alternative seating options. If a child has anxiety, their 504 plan might include extra time to complete assignments and regular check-ins with the guidance counselor. If a child has a mild reading disability, their 504 plan might include access to audiobooks and text-to-speech technology. In each of these examples, the student is still expected to meet the demands of the curriculum in the general education classroom.

Overall, students and parents have less rights with a 504 plan. There are no specific goals set, no mandated progress monitoring or reporting, and fewer procedural safeguards. Compared to an IEP, there is much less accountability placed on the school district to meet your child's individual needs. Although it is best practice, parents aren't required to be in attendance at the meetings to develop and review a 504 plan. In fact, they don't even need to be invited.

CHAPTER 7
Creation of the IEP

IEPs across the country have the same basic components. The appearance of the document varies greatly from state to state, district to district though. One thing we can all agree upon is that these things aren't exactly parent-friendly, and they're definitely not page-turners! Reading an IEP from start to finish takes a special kind of patience. Even if they are able to get through the whole thing, most parents tell me they have no idea what they just read. There is an abundance of jargon and way too many words jammed onto each page.

Some of the IEPs I've seen remind me of the instructions that come with purchases from IKEA—the Swedish version! Or the single-spaced liability waiver that parents have to sign at the trampoline park. Be honest. Have any of you out there ever done the same blah, blah, blah, sign at the bottom routine with your child's IEP and called it a day? It's all right. I won't tell. If I'm being honest, I can't totally blame you.

But let's change that starting today, okay?

Myths about IEPs

If you take a closer look at the public school education roadmap, you'll see that there isn't one General Education Highway and one Special Education Highway. Nope, all of our children are driving on the same Route K12. All students are moving toward the same high school graduation finish line. Some vehicles are going to get customized to varying degrees along the way though. Whatever a student with a disability needs to make forward progress at an appropriate rate is what the district is legally required to provide, at no cost to the parents.

There is one critical caveat though . . . your public school district has no obligation to provide your child with a blinged-out Rolls Royce! This is a difficult pill for many parents to swallow, because of course, we want our children to have the BEST of everything, right? But nope, you won't find the word *best* written anywhere in the IDEA with respect to educational quality. You will find the word *appropriate* plenty of times though. Specifically, your district is required to provide an appropriate education that meets your child's needs and prepares them for "further education, employment, and independent living . . ." So, you can expect a much more modest, efficient, and reliable vehicle to be designed for your child. In the *Rowley* case, a historic special education court ruling from 1982, the judge compared the standard for public schools to a "Serviceable Chevrolet." When I'm talking to parents today, I tell them to expect something along the lines of a Honda Accord.

Another misconception we can clear up right away is that special education is a place. It isn't. When people use the phrase "in special education," it rubs me the wrong way every time. It suggests that there is a physical space, a container of sorts, for children with disabilities. The truth is, special education is a *service*, not a place. A broad umbrella of services and supports actually. It's an array of educational strategies, resources, and environments carefully crafted to the individual needs of each student. Every single IEP should be uniquely designed and one of a kind. Just like each child.

The Special Education Backbone

I want to make sure you have clarity around two fundamental IEP truths.

#1: Your child's NEEDS determine their GOALS.

#2: Your child's GOALS determine the SPECIALLY DESIGNED INSTRUCTION they receive.

The relationship is perfectly linear so you can think of it like this:

Needs ⇨ Goals ⇨ Specially Designed Instruction

This flowchart is the backbone of the IEP. We'll add a few more pieces in this chapter too. You'd be shocked at how many times I see breakdowns in this basic structure when I'm first reviewing a student's education plan. In defense of school teams, it's super easy to lose sight of the forest for the trees; to get so caught up in the day-to-day details that we forget about the big picture. I encourage you to keep coming back to this chapter as a reference, especially when it's annual review time.

Present Levels of Academic Achievement and Functional Performance

I would argue that the **Present Levels** is the most important section of the IEP because it describes the extent to which a child's disability is affecting their school performance. Evaluation results, grades, standardized test scores, and educator summaries are all gathered here.

You want to make very certain that ALL of your child's areas of need are captured in detail. Why? Look at your backbone again. Identified needs lead directly to the creation of individualized goals. For every single need, a corresponding goal should be written. And from there, specially designed instruction is chosen. In a nutshell, if you want the school to provide instruction to help your child improve their skills in a particular area, make sure their present level of functioning in that domain is accurately documented in the IEP.

Can you see how the Present Levels section is fueled directly by the evaluation phase of the IEP process, as well as ongoing curriculum-based assessments? And how important it is that your child is evaluated in ALL areas of suspected disability? Every step is connected and interdependent. We could even add a few more pieces to the front end of our IEP diagram, like this:

Evaluations ⇨ Present Levels ⇨ Needs ⇨ Goals ⇨ Specially Designed Instruction

So how does all of this apply to advocating for our kiddos in real life? Here are a few examples that I hope will drive it home for you.

If you want the school to help your child become a better reader, have their phonological awareness, decoding, fluency, and comprehension skills been evaluated thoroughly? Is their current performance in each area described in Present Levels? If not, ask the teacher to update the IEP with this information. The only way to measure progress is to know exactly where a student is starting from.

If you want the school to help your child with functional living skills, such as tying shoes, toileting, and washing hands, their present levels of functioning in these areas should have been measured. Were they? Are the results included in Present Levels? If not, make a request that the information be added.

If you want your child to receive support for their anxiety in the form of accommodations and regular sessions with the school counselor, has information about how it's presenting in the classroom been collected? A diagnosis from a mental health professional is often a helpful piece of the puzzle, but there are also various parent, student, and teacher rating scales that can be used. A school team cannot diagnose your child with anxiety, BUT they can measure the extent to which it's impacting educational performance.

Goals and Objectives

Well-written goals are the guideposts, or mile markers, along your child's educational journey. Goals ensure that your child's "car" and everyone in it are moving in the right direction, at the correct pace. If carefully followed, a driver will never have to worry about losing their way. **Objectives** are the smaller actions and behaviors that go into achieving the larger goal.

Goals are written based on the child's unique learning profile and present levels of achievement. They describe a reasonable amount of growth that can be expected in *one year*. The balance between being both realistic and sufficiently rigorous is a tricky one. "Ambitious but achievable" goals are the standard that I encourage parents to advocate for.

IEP goals should be SMART. I've seen this acronym broken down in several different ways, but here is my favorite. I've included the key questions that you should be asking yourself when reading each goal in your child's IEP.

S = Specific

Does this goal sound generic or like it was written specifically for your child? Is the goal vague, or does it pinpoint a specific skill?

Generic goals are extremely common and a huge pet peeve of mine. Most IEP software programs today have a pull-down menu from which teachers and case managers select pre-written goals from a bank. Now that doesn't sound very individualized to you, does it? Believe me, I do understand the need for convenience. Speaking from experience, writing high-quality goals is not easy. It's a skill that develops over time with lots of practice and trial and error. But cookie-cutter IEPs are not serving our children. If your school team tells you that they cannot include a specific goal because it's not listed in their pull-down menu, that's a major red flag. There should always be the ability to customize goals and craft them from scratch if necessary. Even if it involves writing it into the document by hand!

M = Measurable

Can data be collected for this goal? Can progress be measured and quantified?

I often see "teacher report" or "teacher observation" listed as broad methods for data collection. Unfortunately, these phrases are incredibly vague and often fail to produce the cold, hard indicators needed to evaluate progress. In order to measure the progress of a child toward a goal, there needs to be baseline data taken at the beginning of the year, and then additional data collected at regular intervals after that. Parents can and should literally ask to see the numbers. Are they going up? Trending downward? Staying the same? The only way to determine the effectiveness of instruction is to monitor progress in a very deliberate manner like this. If growth is not taking place, it's time for an increase in intervention or a new instructional approach altogether.

A = Attainable

Is this goal realistic? Can it be achieved by the end of the IEP (one year)?

Hear me out on this one. Do I think that the goals children with disabilities are working on should be written with state standards of proficiency for that grade level in mind? Absolutely. It's essential that the IEP Team is always mindful of where we want a student to ultimately end up. I'm a HUGE believer in high expectations and continually raising the bar for teachers and students alike. BUT, if a fourth-grader is reading at a first-grade level, is it appropriate for all of their reading goals to be taken directly from the grade level standards? Should a decoding goal start with the words, "When reading texts at the 4th grade level…"? Probably not. How about including goals that target the specific skills the child needs to acquire in order to close this gap? This is a much more effective approach, and one that parents can advocate for.

R = Relevant

Is the goal related to the ultimate goal of preparing the student for post-secondary life? Is it aligned with the grade level curriculum? Does the goal address one of the most pressing areas of need?

Every single academic and functional need documented in the Present Levels section should have a corresponding goal. I encourage parents to comb through the Present Levels section and all evaluations performed very carefully. With a highlighter, mark every single time your child struggled or scored below grade level norms. Does the IEP have a goal connected to this need? It should!

One quick caveat here. For children with very high levels of need, their IEPs could contain an extremely long list of goals. As an IEP Team, you're going to have to prioritize what's most important at that moment in time. By selecting a reasonable number of goals for that school year, some areas of need might not be addressed until future IEPs. In my opinion, that's both logical and acceptable.

T = Time-bound

Is the goal written for the year? Are objectives broken down further by marking period or semester?

IEP goals are expected to be achieved within one year since that is the duration of the IEP. If a student meets the goal prior to the one-year mark, even better! The team can then come together to amend the IEP and put a new, more challenging goal in its place. For each goal, there should also be mention of how often progress will be assessed and reported back to parents. Typically, this will coincide with report cards. I've even seen the objectives under some goals broken down by marking period. This makes it easier for teachers and parents to track progress throughout the year.

* * *

As someone who has had firsthand experience, goal-writing is not always easy. I challenge you to take a look at the goals and objectives in your child's IEP. Each and every one. Are they clearly written? Do they pass the SMART test?

Do not hesitate to ask the school team to rewrite any goals that don't meet these standards. But, also be prepared to offer some suggestions of your own. Remember, it's all about collaboration. Technically, the IEP Team should be writing the goals together. Do some research ahead of time and familiarize yourself with what SMART goals look and sound like. There are literally hundreds of resources about goal writing out there in internet-land. Some are better than others. Many sites even house IEP goal banks separated by grade level and performance area. Use the examples you find as a starting point and then spend some time customizing them for your child.

Special Education

This is the part of the IEP that explicitly states everything your child "gets." It's a description of the specialized instruction, services, technology, accommodations, modifications, and any other support the IEP Team determines your child needs. Technically, these decisions should be among the last that the team makes.

Remember how the student's needs and goals must be clearly established first? If you ever sit down to an Annual Review IEP Meeting and the very first item on the agenda is your child's program for the following year, that's another red flag.

Needs ⇨ Goals ⇨ Specially Designed Instruction

Related Services are needed to help a child benefit from specialized instruction. Some examples of related services include occupational therapy, physical therapy, speech therapy, counseling, nurse services, and transportation. Details about the type, frequency, duration, and location of each are spelled out in this section of the IEP.

Some examples of **supplementary aids and services** include a 1:1 aide, specialized training for staff and/or parents, consultation with related service providers, **assistive technology** (word processor, spell-check device, augmentative communication, special software, etc.), adapted equipment, and peer tutoring. This section also includes the services a child needs to fully participate in nonacademic and extracurricular settings. For example, if your child requires a 1:1 aide throughout the school day, one must be provided during lunch, electives, field trips, as well as after-school clubs, dances, and other school functions.

When determining placement, the team must always consider a continuum of options. The goal here is to identify your child's **least restrictive environment (LRE)**. In other words, the setting that allows greatest access to their non-disabled peers while still providing all of the needed instruction, services, and support.

When a child is educated outside the general education classroom for even a portion of the school day, it's defined as more "restrictive." The IEP Team should consider this only if, ". . . education in regular classes with the use of supplementary aids and services cannot be achieved satisfactorily," per 20 U.S.C. § 1412(a)(5)(A). Settings should be discussed in order from least to most restrictive, according to this list:

- General education classroom
- General education classroom with the in-class support of a special education teacher
- Resource room (small group instruction that is subject-specific and delivered by a special education teacher)
- Self-contained classroom (special education setting for the majority of the school day)
- Special education program within another public school district
- Private school for children with disabilities
- Home instruction

A student's classroom type and placement is subject to change as their needs change. Like the rest of the IEP, decisions about placement are made annually, if not more frequently. We will talk more in-depth about this topic in chapter 20.

Modifications versus Accommodations

The distinction between accommodations and modifications is an important one. **Modifications** are changes to instructional methods, content, and assessment. IEP **accommodations** are more minor tweaks that allow a student with a disability to access the curriculum. I mentioned it already, but it's worth repeating. Accommodations do not change WHAT is being taught, but rather HOW the information is being presented.

Going back to our automobile analogy, *modifications* could mean an entirely different car (bigger, smaller, different make/model, etc.) or any other physical change made to the vehicle the student started with. A different type of tire, additional technology, brighter headlights, and a more powerful engine are a few examples. When applied to learning, modifications include quizzes that cover different or less content than grade-level peers, alternative textbooks and lessons, and specialized instruction that is targeted to the child's learning style. Sometimes the entire curriculum itself changes in order to meet the child's needs.

Accommodations, on the other hand, are strategies to support the driver on his or her journey. For example, moving the seat up/back, repeating the driving directions more frequently and more clearly, checking in regularly with the driver to make sure they know where they're going, lowering the radio volume to limit distractions, prepping the driver before they get going each day, and more frequently scheduled oil changes. The car itself hasn't been "modified" significantly at all. Rather, settings have been adjusted to allow full access to the open road. The student behind the wheel will be much better equipped to navigate around any barriers placed in their path.

I like to think of most accommodations simply as good teaching—strategies that most teachers I know would try anyway if they noticed a student was struggling. Some common examples are allowing a student extra time to complete a task, highlighting the directions on worksheets and quizzes, frequent check-ins for understanding, seating a child close to the teacher, and providing more white space between questions on a math test. The possibilities are truly endless. Don't hesitate to offer your own suggestions to the team. Better yet, ask your child what he or she thinks would help them learn more easily, and then ask for it to be included as an accommodation.

* * *

The parents who contact me do so when their child's IEP isn't working. Often, meaningful progress is not being made because either the proper supports and services aren't in place, or they're not being implemented with fidelity. Basically, the public school system handed these children a lemon. As you can imagine, the parents are not only worried, they're fuming. Wouldn't you be?

Maybe a child hasn't been placed in the appropriate educational setting. Or the interventions being utilized are outdated or not research-based. Perhaps a school district is caught up in "but this is how we've always done things" mode. They aren't willing to think outside the box and individualize their solutions. Whatever the circumstances, watching your child's education break down in front of your eyes is heart-wrenching. The vehicle that's supposed to be carrying them safely in the right direction just isn't getting the job done. Instead, it's chugging, sputtering, making lots of loud noises, and on the verge of stranding the driver on the side of the road. These are the cases that demand immediate action by parents.

Now that you've passed Special Education 101, it's time to apply what you've learned and start thinking strategically. You have a solid foundation of knowledge upon which to build, and are ready for more of the good stuff. I'm happy to report that you've come to the right place. Raise your hand if you'd like to pour more fuel into your advocacy tank. I'd love to do the honors.

PART 3

Savvy Advocacy Strategies

• • • ● ● ● ● • •

There are a few essential strategies and "soft skills" that you're going to need in your advocacy toolbox in order to represent your child's interests most effectively. You will make mistakes. And guess what? Your child's teachers will too. If you're playing the long game, you won't get so incredibly stressed about every little detail that needs to be ironed out. You'll take everything in stride and keep moving forward.

Your number one objective is to actively build and nurture a collaborative relationship with your school district. One that is characterized by mutual respect and trust. A relationship that allows you and the rest of the team to problem-solve together productively when problems arise. Trust me on this one!

Also keep in mind that you won't be advocating in a vacuum. The actions you take and decisions you make will often depend on the other members of your child's IEP Team. Personalities, levels of experience, Special Education Department leadership and school culture are all important variables. And let's not forget that your child is changing year to year. So are their needs, attitude toward learning, and the demands that each new school year brings. You're going to have to become really nimble in order to respond accordingly. It's like a game of chess in that the board is always changing. So without further ado, let's talk about some of your best moves.

CHAPTER 8
Develop Your Advocacy Style

....

I think too many of us moms were conditioned very early on to be polite people-pleasers. We have been shaped by cultural messages urging us to be sweet, agreeable "nice girls." But keeping mum is not in our children's best interest when it comes to special education advocacy. On the flip side, women who are more outspoken and direct are at risk of being cast in a negative light. They are unfairly assigned adjectives such as demanding, angry, and difficult. We can't win.

In order to represent yourself in the best manner possible, self-awareness is an important first step. Do you tend to have a hard time voicing your opinion when it differs from the majority? Are you easily intimidated when it comes to school stuff? Have you ever been told that you come on too strong? Do you have a hard time admitting your mistakes? Once you identify your personal strengths and weaknesses, you can make adjustments accordingly. Imagine that you were a fly on the wall during your child's last IEP meeting. Take an honest look at yourself—how would you describe your advocacy style?

The Goldilocks Principle

We're all familiar with the classic fairy tale "Goldilocks and the Three Bears" and her bowls of porridge that are too hot, too cold, and just right. Throughout the story, Goldilocks encounters two extremes and then the sweet spot right in the middle. We can apply this same concept to paint a picture of how an effective advocate thinks and behaves. Do you recognize yourself in any of these? I think the images will resonate.

Type 1: The Pushover

Allow me to introduce you to the pushover. She's a loving mother and gets along swimmingly with everyone she meets; but when it comes to advocating on behalf of her child's learning needs, she just hasn't found her voice.

Instead of being actively involved in the IEP process, the pushover is a mere observer. She brings a tray of homemade cookies to meetings, but has little else to contribute. Pushover parents rarely ask questions, keep input to a bare minimum, and would never dream of ruffling any feathers. Even when problems arise or important decisions need to be made, they remain passive. Pushovers are uber-agreeable and perfectly content to grin and go with the flow.

For the most part, busy school teams love them! IEP meetings are one-sided, short, and sweet. Pushovers sign on the dotted line right at the table, take a copy of the IEP home, and promptly toss it into a drawer where it may never again see the light of day.

I'm sure that the pushover means well. Here's the problem though . . . parents are valuable members of the IEP Team. They know their child better than anyone, so their participation in the IEP process is critical. When moms and dads "show up," it keeps educators on their toes and holds everyone accountable for doing their best work.

Please don't be a pushover.

But pretty please, don't be a gladiator either!

Type 2: The Gladiator

Gladiators are overly aggressive and often trapped in an "us versus them" mindset. They mistakenly believe that there are winners and losers at the IEP table and that it's only after a violent fight to the death that a victor will be the last one standing.

Parents like this are their own worst enemy. They genuinely believe they are helping their child, but instead end up sabotaging the home-school relationship. A confrontational approach is never, ever, in your child's best interest. Gladiators are inflexible, unreasonable, and really struggle with effective communication. Intimidation and threats are their weapons of choice during times of conflict, as opposed to strategic advocacy.

Gladiators often carry preconceived notions about how public schools operate. Sometimes they've had bad experiences in the past and trust has been lost. Or they've heard stories about school districts withholding services from children who need them, due to dollar signs. Gladiators are a cynical bunch. Their guard is up at all times.

I once worked with a mom who contacted me regarding her sweet little girl. Mia came into the world after a complicated pregnancy and delivery. Now as a preschooler, she was exhibiting developmental delays and sensory needs. At home, Mia was a handful. She tore around the house like a tornado and had a hard time following directions. Mom wanted help in advocating for a private school placement for children with disabilities.

From our very first conversation on the phone, I got the impression that she was gearing up for a fight. In fact, she used that exact word a handful of times as we formulated a game plan. She also used phrases like "not letting them see all of our cards" and was adamant about keeping some of Mia's private evaluations under wraps. I tried to make the case for transparency, but Mom wasn't convinced.

At the IEP meeting, her tone was brusque and slightly hostile at times. In contrast, the teachers and therapists seemed responsive and collaborative. They maintained that Mia was not a behavior problem in her self-contained classroom. She followed instructions, and most importantly, was making good academic progress. They felt very confident about their ability to meet her needs. Mom was highly skeptical, and told me afterward that the district was just looking to save money by keeping her in their program.

Mom agreed to let me visit the classroom as a neutral observer so I could give her an unbiased report about what was taking place. What I saw was two hours of pure poetry. Mia was engaged, happy, well-behaved, socializing with her peers, and following classroom routines with no difficulty whatsoever. The teacher was masterful.

When I called Mom on the way home, I was thrilled to share how beautifully her baby girl was doing in school! I raved about the teacher and aides, and told her that I would gladly allow my own child to be in that classroom if given the chance. Instead of mirroring back my joy though, she actually seemed disappointed. I was so confused. Wasn't my report music to her ears? I thought about Mom's journey as a single mother, in and out of family court with her ex-husband, and struggling to make ends meet. I think she was so accustomed to conflict and struggle that the concept of trusting the system was a foreign one.

You see, once you have a Gladiator mindset, it's really hard to shake it. I implore you to try though. When you do fall down a rabbit hole of anger or pessimism, do whatever it takes to claw your way out as quickly as possible. Give the benefit of the doubt. If you discover that you were way off base about something, own it. Put your pride aside. Start with a sincere apology, and watch how quickly your humility puts the home-school relationship back on track.

Type 3: The Savvy Advocate

Savvy advocates are "just right." They are collaborative, and intentional about maintaining positive relationships with school personnel. But they're not naive. They understand that differences of opinion are inevitable, so they gather an arsenal of negotiation tools to help communicate their point of view. Savvy advocates have strong interpersonal skills, hold reasonable expectations, and understand the art of compromise. This is the ideal parent advocacy style and the one I want you to emulate.

Savvy advocates are educated. They are confident in their knowledge of their children, their learning profile, and their rights under IDEA. They communicate clearly and directly, and don't apologize when asking questions or requesting additional information for clarification. At the same time, they respect the expertise of others. Savvy advocates recognize that educators are the experts when it comes to instruction, intervention, the classroom environment, and how children perform inside of it. They believe that educators are inherently good people.

Savvy advocates are transparent. They don't have a hidden agenda. They are solution-oriented, and not interested in playing the blame game. Savvy advocates are optimists. They believe every problem can be solved, even if it means that some out-of-the-box thinking is required.

So where do you see yourself along the advocacy continuum? More of a softy or more savvy? Like you could have held your own against Russell Crowe in the Colosseum back in the day? Too passive, too aggressive, or just right?

Emotional Blinders

When it comes to our children, it's nearly impossible for emotions not to come into play. It's how mamas are made. We're wired to protect and defend at all costs. We meet perceived threats with aggression. We stand up on our hind legs and we roar. We bare our teeth and ready our claws. The mama bears of cubs who are struggling or vulnerable in some way are the most fierce.

This characteristic doesn't always lend itself to productive discussion at the IEP table though. Intense emotion can prevent us from looking at the facts of the matter and problem-solving objectively. Emotions are like blinders. Once your bloodstream gets flooded with stress hormones like cortisol and adrenaline, it's impossible to think rationally. You're no longer able to process new information coming in, nor advocate effectively.

So what should you do if you find yourself in this predicament? Take a breather. Literally. If you're in the middle of a meeting, request a 5-minute break to collect yourself. Walk outside to get fresh air, or head to the bathroom to splash some cold water on your face. Enjoy a few deep breaths, and don't beat yourself up for losing your cool. We're all human. If necessary, ask to end the meeting early and reconvene at a later time when emotions have subsided.

I've cried at my own children's IEP meetings before. I've had tense conversations with teachers and case managers. It's not something I'm proud of, but it's also not the end of the world. Have you ever noticed that there are tissue boxes on most IEP tables? It's not a coincidence. As hard as you try to stay calm, cool, and collected, emotions can find a way to creep in. Give yourself grace. Tomorrow is a new day.

Mending Broken Bridges

Sometimes when I first start working with a family, I encounter a messy situation. Damage has already been done, trust has been broken, and communication is at a standstill. I typically ask the parent to forward me the last few email correspondences that have been exchanged. I cringe when I discover language from parents that is harsh and downright insulting. How in the world did things get to this point? Furthermore, what can be done to get the relationship back on track?

Mom to mom, I've been there. I've felt backed into a corner and powerless. When the IEP Team says no, it feels so final. You can walk out of a meeting feeling completely defeated, and at the risk of sounding dramatic, violated. The "fight" doesn't seem fair. Lashing out feels like your only option.

But no matter how frustrated you feel, hurling accusations or even worse, making personal attacks, is never going to end well. Once the words are hanging in the air or sitting in someone's inbox, you can never get them back. If you need to vent, find a friend. Write the ugliest, nastiest, profanity-laden email that you can. Name names, and throw them all under the bus. Get everything off your chest. But instead of hitting send, hit delete. Unloading all of your angst can feel cathartic, therapeutic even. So do it! But please do it safely.

When discussions reach an impasse and a mutually agreed upon solution simply cannot be reached, this is when your advocacy skills really come into play. The antidote to feeling helpless is to take action. The fact of the matter is that parents are NOT powerless when it comes to special education. There is so much more that you CAN do to advocate for your child's needs. So roll up your sleeves and get to work!

Start with a genuine apology. Own any behavior that was less than respectful, and promise that it's never going to happen again. Express your sincere desire to get back on track and work together more collaboratively moving forward. State that you are willing to compromise and are open to finding creative solutions that satisfy all parties. You can do all of this via a carefully worded email, or request a face-to-face meeting to ensure that there is no miscommunication.

One word that I want you to keep in mind when you're advocating is the magic word *reasonable*. Is what you're asking a teacher to do for your child reasonable? Or is it a request that will be nearly impossible for him or her to fulfill? Like in any human relationship, one side isn't going to "get their way" every time. I'm reluctant to use this next analogy because collaboration and negotiation shouldn't feel like warfare, but I think it will help drive home the point. Parents need to be willing to compromise during the smaller "skirmishes" that aren't as critical in the scheme of the larger "war." Choose your battles wisely.

At the end of the day, it's in your child's best interest to have a positive working relationship with school personnel. Period. You don't have to be holding hands and singing Kumbaya in the conference room, but there needs to be a line of respect and professionalism that is never crossed. To the greatest extent possible, savvy parents check their emotions at the door and advocate from a place of calm, focused, rational confidence. You can too.

CHAPTER 9

Communicate Effectively

At my bridal shower, the guests who had been married the longest were invited to share their best advice for a happy marriage. There was one nugget of wisdom that kept getting repeated over and over again: Communication is everything.

This truth applies to ALL relationships, if you think about it. Friendships, family relationships, work relationships, and the one between parents and special education teams. Your ability to express yourself clearly, and listen to alternative points of view, is critical. Communication is the oil that greases all of the parts under the hood and keeps the education vehicle running smoothly.

If I had to guess, I would estimate that over 80 percent of the conflict between school teams and parents could easily be avoided with better communication. By the time I typically get involved, things have already taken a turn for the worse. Even so, the majority of the time, we are able to right the ship. It never ceases to amaze me how a single face-to-face meeting can get everyone back on the same page again.

Effective communication is a cornerstone of savvy advocacy. This one soft skill is so gosh-darn important that I'm devoting an entire chapter to it! Some parents have a natural knack for it, while others struggle mightily. But the great news is, there are a few best practices that are tried-and-true.

The Snowball Effect

Many issues in the special education world start with a relatively tiny breakdown in communication that grows bigger and bigger over time. One misinterpreted statement in an email, comment on a child's paper, or remark at a conference can quickly spiral out of control. I call it the snowball effect.

If no one intervenes to set the record straight, something that starts out completely innocuous can take on a life of its own. It can happen very quickly, and have a devastating impact on everyone involved. Inevitably, the negative fallout trickles down to the very person you're trying to protect in the first place—your child. Gulp.

Let's take a closer look from both perspectives, since communication is a two-way street.

There are times when a parent feels like they're not being heard. Their questions and concerns keep getting brushed aside. Parents get the impression that the school doesn't support them. All the work they're doing to advocate for their child is being misinterpreted. They feel outnumbered and get frustrated.

But the reverse is also true. And remarkably similar.

There are times when an educator feels like they're not being heard. Their professional expertise keeps getting brushed aside. Educators get the impression that the parents don't support them. All the work they're doing to help their students is being ignored. They feel underappreciated and get defensive.

Uh-oh.

Can you see how easy it is for the parent-educator relationship to become strained? For trust to be broken? I've personally experienced it from both sides and can vouch for the fact that they feel equally miserable. Sometimes it's the *lack* of consistent communication that causes the most damage. The following scenario actually happened to one of my families and illustrates it perfectly.

Imagine you're a conscientious parent who is eager to determine the most appropriate placement for your son with autism. He will be transitioning to high school next year, so you want to get it right. You've been asking your case manager to arrange tours of various programs in the area since October. Now it's May. Your child will be graduating from eighth grade in less than a month, and everything is still up in the air. You are officially in panic mode.

You sent yet another email reminder to your case manager on Monday morning that still hasn't been responded to. It's now Thursday. In the span of those four days, your thoughts and emotions have been all over the place. Here's an honest snapshot.

<u>Doubt and regret</u>:

Was my email too harsh?

Are they annoyed that I keep bugging them?

Am I "that parent" who is being overly demanding?

<u>Anxiety</u>:

Will I ever hear back?

What if all the spots in the best schools get taken?

Big transitions are hard for my son. I need to start preparing him ASAP!

<u>Anger</u>:

What the hell????

How long does it take to reply to a simple email?

This is totally rude and unprofessional.

<u>Disappointment</u>:

I can't count on them.

I'm all alone in this.

The school doesn't care about my child or family.

<u>Defeat</u>:

What am I supposed to do now?

I feel totally helpless.

This process feels so unfair.

Talk about an emotional roller coaster. In this particular case, the case manager was a historically poor communicator. Her lack of responsiveness strained their relationship time and time again. So many conflicts and misunderstandings could have—and should have—been avoided. Ultimately, tours were hastily arranged in the final hour and a placement was agreed upon. It's unfortunate that the parent's road to get to that point was so stressful though. They didn't deserve that.

The reality is that parents cannot control all of the variables when it comes to communication. There are too many other players involved. But what you CAN control are your own words, behaviors, and responses. With this in mind, I have four rules of thumb that have always served me well. I call them the Communication Commandments.

The Communication Commandments

1) Thou shalt be proactive.

At the beginning of each school year, make it a priority to open up a positive line of communication with your child's teachers and therapists. I recommend scheduling either a parent-teacher conference or a full IEP meeting about 4–6 weeks into the school year. By that time, the team will have gotten to know your child, and they'll be better prepared to share meaningful insight. The first few weeks of the year are a whirlwind. Teachers are working diligently to learn about each student and establish classroom routines. That is not the time to pepper them with too many specifics about your child. By the 6-week mark though, things have settled down. The honeymoon period is over and the nitty-gritty work has begun.

The key here is to start communicating with your child's teacher BEFORE a problem arises. I don't advise waiting until the end of the first grading period. When you get more of a jumpstart, you're laying an important foundation upon which a successful school year can be built.

There should be two goals for that very first meeting.

First, you want to make their IEP or 504 plan come alive. Your child is so much more than a stapled packet of paper, aren't they? Your child is so much more than their special education classification and test scores, yes? This is your chance to paint a picture of the living, breathing, learning, growing, shining human child behind it all.

I recommend creating a Student Snapshot and bringing copies to the meeting with you. In the Appendix, you can see a copy of the simple template that I used for my sixth-grader last year. When I handed them out to his teachers when we met in early October, the feedback was extremely positive. To quote his Math teacher, "This is great. I wish all parents did this!"

The IEP is supposed to be strengths-based, but it often feels like the child's needs take center stage. Here's your opportunity to share information about his or her interests, passions, and preferred activities. Not only is this incredibly useful for teachers looking to motivate or make a personal connection with your child, but it also keeps the focus on them as a whole person. The trick is to keep the Snapshot short and sweet. Think bullet points, phrases, and only the most important nuggets of information. I advise no more than three bullet points for each section. Remember, you're trying to majorly simplify the IEP, not create another one.

Instead of a teacher or therapist taking weeks or even months to really get to know your child, you've streamlined the process for them. Time is a precious commodity in the world of special education. Every minute of every day counts.

You'll definitely want to share the strategies and methods that worked best for your child last year. This is priceless information. If it's not broken, don't fix it. The new teachers will put their own spin on it, but if there is something that your child responded to particularly well, definitely mention it. In an ideal world there is airtight, direct communication between teachers from grade level to grade level. But in my experience, this is more the exception than the rule. Especially if a student is transitioning to a new school and/or working with a new case manager. Inevitably, information will slip through the cracks. This is your chance to mitigate the damage.

The second priority of that initial meeting is to establish an ongoing system of communication that works for all parties. You should inquire about each educator's preferred method—email? Phone call? Handwritten notes in a communication journal? How often should you expect to hear from them? How often will progress be reported?

Ask how long it typically takes for them to reply to parent messages, so you know how long to wait before you follow up. This accomplishes a few things. It sets the tone that you are respectful of their time and that you wish to establish a close working relationship.

2) Thou shalt express gratitude.

I'm sure you've heard the expression, "You catch more flies with honey than vinegar." It's so cliché, but it's never been more true than in education advocacy. As a parent, you're far more likely to attract better outcomes if you are more sweet than sour with school staff. It behooves you to make the conscious decision to insert positivity, praise, and gratitude into every interaction.

You might be breathing a big sigh of relief because you've managed to avoid teacher and IEP conflict up to this point. Overall, you're pleased with the education your child is receiving and the professionals delivering it. So you should just sit back contentedly and enjoy it, right? Well, by all means, please do that. BUT, if that's all you do, you would be missing out on a wonderful opportunity for gratitude. By taking the time to let the school team know how thankful you are, you are reinforcing their effort and increasing the likelihood that it will continue. Yup, I want you to make it a priority to serve up some honey with a side of sunshine on the regular.

No matter how contentious or complicated a situation might already be, I start every single communication, both written and face-to-face, with an expression of gratitude. Every. Single. Time. It doesn't have to be over the top, but it should be sincere. Here are a few simple examples.

At the beginning of a meeting/phone call:

"Thank you so much for taking the time to call this morning. I know it's an extra busy time of the day."

"I want to start the meeting by saying thank you for helping Chase feel so comfortable in your class this year. He loves coming to school each day."

"I really appreciate that you were able to gather everyone together to talk about Emma this afternoon."

At the beginning of an email:

"I want to thank you very much for talking to Jamie and his friends during recess today. He feels so much better now."

"Thank you for following up with me about this so quickly."

"I appreciate you reaching out to let me know that Jasmine had a rough morning."

Appreciation is always going to be well-received. It sends the message that you desire collaboration and you're not there simply to complain or nitpick. Newsflash . . . some parents are! Which explains why many school teams approach conversations with parents with their guard up. Gratitude is powerful. It's a bridge builder and a tension diffuser. Saying thank you also casts you in a more favorable light. It paints you as an ally, a team player. As the cherry on top, it also makes them feel pretty darn good inside.

I try to end all of my interactions with this same principle in mind. No matter how tense a meeting becomes, or how serious your concerns in an email are, always strive to end on a positive note. Gratitude is the tool to help you do just that.

At the end of a meeting/phone call:

"Thank you for meeting with me today. Even though we don't agree on this particular issue, I appreciate your willingness to consider my viewpoint."

"Thank you for answering all of my questions, and explaining the evaluations so thoroughly."

"Thank you for all that you do for Madison every day."

At the end of an email:

"Thank you for being open to my input and thank you in advance for any additional suggestions that you have."

"I greatly appreciate the extra time you're taking to help Jalen each day."

"Thank you again for reaching out with your concerns. I look forward to working together to help Chase have a successful year."

Teachers are overworked, underpaid, and experiencing high rates of burnout. There are no cash bonuses awarded for high performance, no trophies for writing the best IEPs, and no tropical vacations for the educator who changed the most lives that year. So, if you're sitting at the IEP table and have the chance to thank someone who has made a difference in the life of your child, by all means, GO FOR IT! To offer a specific compliment to an educator in front of their colleagues would make their day. Heck, it would probably make their year. Verbal praise is a powerful love language for many. It's pretty amazing what even a single serving of the sweet stuff can do.

3) Thou shalt remain professional and courteous.

I'll reference another piece of timeless wisdom for my next commandment. Have you ever heard the expression, "It's not what you say but HOW you say it?" This old adage holds true for almost all situations in life, including those that are IEP-related. Even when your emotions have been triggered, keep your written and oral communication style as professional as possible.

Email is a wonderful thing . . . most of the time. We live during a time when it's never been easier to stay in contact with school personnel. But for all of the benefits that modern technology offers, the biggest drawback is the very real potential for miscommunication. I mean, who hasn't been on the sending or receiving end of a digital message that has been misconstrued? Before you know it, an innocent email or text has taken on a life of its own and damaged relationships.

When advocating for your child, the tone of all written communication should be polite, yet assertive. You want to state your viewpoints and requests clearly while remaining respectful. Real talk—if you're angry or upset about something, this is going to take a heck of a lot of restraint on your part. You're rarely going to hit send on your first draft of an email. You may have to go back and reread what you wrote several times to tone things down.

Have your spouse or a trusted friend take a look and offer constructive criticism. Make revisions by softening the language, adding opening and closing lines of gratitude, and backing up your points with specific examples. At no time should your written communication come across as demanding, rude, insulting, passive aggressive, or threatening in any way. Once you go there, you've weakened your argument. And let's not forget that hostile emails can be used against you as evidence in an administrative hearing, if it ever gets to that point. Please choose your words very carefully.

4) Thou shalt be reasonable.

Teachers are BUSIER THAN BUSY.

The reality is that they're squeezing parent emails and phone calls into short, 40-minute "prep" blocks in which they're expected to accomplish a zillion other tasks too. These tiny, precious windows of time are also for making photocopies, grading papers, collaborating with colleagues, and preparing for the next lesson. On a good day, they might even get a few seconds to use the restroom or gobble down a granola bar for lunch. And let's think for a second about the quality of teacher responses that we expect to receive. It takes time to write a thoughtful, meaningful email to a parent.

Simply put, there aren't enough hours in the day. If I had a magic wand, I would grant each teacher a paid "communication hour" in which they could focus exclusively on the ever-so-important communication piece of the job. But until that happens, it's vital that we are reasonable with our expectations and grant educators the benefit of the doubt whenever possible.

Trust me when I say, you don't want to be "that" parent. That parent who is overly demanding and unrealistic with their expectations. That parent who sends multiple emails on multiple days in a row. That parent who doesn't give the teacher a reasonable amount of time to address a situation fully. That parent who never has anything complimentary to say. That parent who thinks, speaks, or types in a disrespectful manner. There is a monumental difference between strong, savvy advocacy and bullying. Please don't get the two confused.

I've seen the fallout from poor parent behavior and it's not pretty. It can even end up damaging your reputation in the school district, for all of your children, for years to come. It's not uncommon for administrators to try to protect their staff from harassment by advising them to cease all communication with "difficult" parents. From that point forward, parent-teacher correspondence is filtered through a case manager or department supervisor. While this strategy is infuriating for parents and makes communication about day-to-day matters extremely challenging, I am empathetic to the reasoning behind it. My hope for you is that you never find yourself in this position.

Imagine that your child's IEP states that study guides are to be provided to help prepare for tests and quizzes. According to your sixth-grader, he wasn't given one for the first two science quizzes of the year. He's upset about his poor grades and you're angry at the teacher for not following his IEP. What should you do? Let's compare two parent emails, written very differently.

Parent A:

Mr. Allen,

I'm extremely disappointed that you're not following Jimmy's IEP. That's illegal and irresponsible of you. You've set my child up for failure, and now he's experiencing major test anxiety. If you don't fix this situation ASAP, I will be contacting your principal and the Board of Education.

Parent B:

Hello Mr. Allen,

I hope your school year is off to a good start. I was reviewing Jimmy's IEP last night and was reminded that study guides are listed as an accommodation. I haven't seen any from Science class, so perhaps Jimmy is misplacing them between home and school. Have study guides been provided? Jimmy was very upset about his first two quiz grades and I'm concerned that his anxiety is going to flare up as a result. Thank you in advance for any clarity you can offer.

Can you hear the difference? Isn't it night and day? Which one do you think is more likely to produce the desired result? Which one is more likely to result in a sincere apology and improved accountability? Which one is more likely to jeopardize the parent-teacher relationship? Which one is going to interfere with your ability to be an effective advocate for your child in the long run?

Trust me, I'm not naive to the real challenges that parents face when working with educators. I realize there are going to be moments when your ability to remain professional is tested. There are going to be case managers and teachers who push your buttons. There are going to be seasons in your life when you're not capable of taking a step back and keeping your emotions in check. There are going to be times when you've made a request for the fifth time and still, nothing has changed. You're only human, and patience can wear thin.

When the high road approach isn't working and you feel like your child's educational rights are being violated, there are much more aggressive advocacy steps you can take to bring change. Definitely keep reading if this is your situation. When it comes to day-to-day correspondence though, these four commandments will save the day.

Consistent Systems

In some situations, daily communication between parents and educators is warranted. Particularly for younger children and those with more complex educational, behavioral, or medical needs. I recommend a *communication notebook* for this purpose. It doesn't have to be fancy at all; a simple notebook that goes back and forth in your child's backpack will do. In it, parents and teachers can exchange information about everything from toileting and sleep issues to medication changes and homework. The continuity of messaging and expectations is extremely powerful, especially for kiddos who thrive on consistency.

With solid communication systems in place, students learn very quickly that all of the adults in their life are on the same page and working together as a team.

A daily checklist of activities and behavior monitoring sheets are two alternatives to the communication notebook. These tools can be easily customized to the student's needs and help with data collection too. A *checklist* is more like a timeline of what the child is doing each day in school. Teachers keep track of activities as they are completed and assign "scores" for things like effort and behavior. Over time, patterns are likely to emerge which can be used to inform future instruction.

Behavior monitoring sheets are useful when specific behaviors are being targeted for extinction or reinforcement. I've seen everything from numbers, colors, and emojis to phrases like "Great job!" "On the right track," and "Improvement needed" used to document progress. The details will depend on the child, their interests, and age level. As children get older, *self-monitoring* becomes an increasingly important skill for them to learn. When they're ready, they can start to take ownership of their behavior by rating themselves throughout the day. Sheets are sent home for a parent signature, so home-school communication is seamless. Parents may even choose to give consequences and rewards at home based on school performance.

Most parents I work with desire more communication than is currently being provided. They're not looking to make extra work for the teacher, but rather, are seeking more involvement in their child's education. Parental involvement is one of the foundational cornerstones of IDEA. In fact, it's mentioned numerous times. The rights of parents to participate in all aspects of IEP decision-making are guaranteed and protected, so don't hesitate to use that argument when advocating for increased communication.

For children who have a communication-based disability, you can imagine how many of their parents feel completely in the dark about how their baby is spending six hours each day. But let's face it; most of our kiddos aren't exactly fountains of information at 4:00 p.m. when we ask, "How was your day?" The three equally dissatisfying answers that I typically hear are, "Fine," "Good," and

"Boring." In response to, "What did you do in school today?" one-word answers are also the norm in my house. I have a strong feeling I'm not alone here. Teacher feedback has always been a lifeline for me for this reason.

Whatever type of communication you're requesting, do what you can to make it as easy as possible for the teacher to implement. For example, if you'd like daily communication, offer to create a template. This way, a teacher can simply circle activities and outcomes that take place, or use check marks on a premade feedback sheet. Shortcuts like these are huge time savers as opposed to expecting a busy teacher to start with a blank page and compose something anecdotal from scratch. If you'd like weekly communication, perhaps you can be the one to initiate a reminder email every Friday morning. That way, your child's teacher can simply reply to it when they get a free moment. Any intentional, collaborative gestures that you make will go a long way in the eyes of your school team. Likewise, they beautifully illustrate your desire to be a true partner in learning.

* * *

Have you ever been in an unfamiliar place when the power goes out? How did it make you feel? Nervous? Frightened? Disoriented? When you're trapped in the dark, your imagination can run wild. It might even conjure up things that aren't really there. Every little noise is magnified and suspicious. Why do you think so many young children worry about monsters in the closet and sleep with the lights on?

When the path we find ourselves on is unlit, every step forward feels uncertain. The same can be said about feeling "in the dark" during your child's special education journey. I hear from parents all the time who are confused and afraid. They feel like they're alone, wandering aimlessly in a foreign land. Improving your communication skills and advocating for more consistent home-school communication are two lanterns that can make a world of difference.

CHAPTER 10
Get Organized

Trees are going to get killed . . . lots of them. You're going to be standing in the middle of a paper blizzard . . . lots of them. If you don't spend some time getting organized, you'll find yourself dazed and confused under a pile of IEPs, evaluation reports, medical records, progress reports, and printed emails. It's not going to be pretty. Trust me, I've been there!

So maybe organization isn't your strong suit, and you're not sure where to even begin. Or, maybe you've tried some methods in the past but nothing has worked well. It's all good! I'm going to make things as simple and as economical as possible for you.

The IEP Binder

From my years spent helping middle school students with ADHD and learning disabilities, I've learned that finding an organization system that works is a highly individual thing. Everyone's brain works a little bit differently. The method I personally find the most useful might drive you bonkers and collect dust in the corner. Trial and error is the name of the game. You might try a system one year, only to find that it needs to be revamped over the summer. That's totally normal. Stay the course.

The most important thing is that you get in the habit of saving everything in one place. In addition to the items already mentioned, you'll also want to save work samples that document areas of concern and evidence of growth. You don't have to keep every single paper that comes home, but hold onto the ones that can be used to bolster your advocacy efforts. For example, if you want your child to get more help with their writing skills, saving assignments in which responses are disorganized and difficult to understand will help you prove your point. Or if you think your eighth-grader is ready for more general education classes in high school, hang on to the most challenging assignments that they ace. All of these things count as data, and are much more powerful than trying to make your argument empty-handed.

Real talk . . . there was one year when life was extra crazy in the Gilliland household. My husband was deployed and I was on my own, juggling potty training, tutoring sessions, doctor appointments, an IEP, and early intervention. It was madness. I felt like I was swimming in an ocean of overwhelm and barely staying afloat. The best I could do was buy a large plastic bin from Target and toss important paperwork for both kids inside. On a good day, I remembered to scribble a date at the top, and in they went. If I needed to find something, I dragged the box out of the corner and rifled through the mess. It was far from perfect, but it was something.

When I got a breather at the end of the school year, I took a few hours on a Sunday afternoon and organized everything chronologically into binders. Survival mode is real. There are going to be seasons in life when the bare minimum is all you can muster. Extend yourself some grace and do what you can. When you have the time and energy to do better, you will.

I recommend investing in a medium-sized binder (1.5 inch) for starters, and a bunch of those plastic page sleeves that you can slide documents into. Generally, one binder per school year, per child, is a good rule of thumb. If it's a year in which your child is reevaluated, an even larger binder might be needed. Each formal evaluation report that you receive is extremely important. They will be used to determine present levels of performance and appropriate IEP goals, so they deserve a prominent place in your records. Start saving and organizing additional information that comes from school chronologically.

If you Google "How to Organize Your Child's IEP Binder" you will find an excellent article from *Understood*, one of my absolute favorite websites for parents. The link even includes a video and several helpful downloads to guide you. The website *A Day in Our Shoes* also has some helpful IEP binder ideas. Pinterest is another great platform to search for organization tips and resources. There is so, so much out there! More than once, I started creating my own systems and templates for parents but then stopped because, why reinvent the wheel? Taking advantage of what already exists is smart and savvy.

Document Everything – The Paper Trail

One of the most popular quotes in education advocacy circles is the classic, "If it's not in writing, it never happened." I'm not sure who gets the original credit, but I heard it for the first time at a Wrightslaw workshop, and have applied it as a best practice ever since. Pete Wright, severe dyslexic, renowned special education attorney and creator of the Wrightslaw website, was discussing the importance of establishing a thorough paper trail.

Essentially, parents should document every single in-person discussion, conference, meeting, and phone call with their child's teachers in writing. Even if it's just an informal chat on the sidewalk at pick-up time. If information about your child's behavior or performance was discussed, jot it down in a designated *IEP notebook* when you get home. Record the date, who you spoke to, and then summarize the main points that were covered. Many parents find it easier to use the Notes section on their phone or create a Google Doc in lieu of a notebook. Go with whatever works best for you. Shoot a quick email back to the person you spoke with, sharing the big takeaways. Otherwise, it may as well have never happened. Without proper documentation, you're going to forget the details of what was shared and promised.

When it comes down to it, what you "remember" someone saying or what you "think" was agreed upon isn't going to hold a ton of weight with a hearing officer. But if you happen to have a notebook with dated entries and detailed summaries, and a follow-up email, it's much more powerful. If you ever have a dispute with your school district, the paper trail you have created will contain valuable pieces of evidence.

Communication via email can be easily printed and added to your child's binder. Your email trail might come into play when you're establishing timelines that need to be adhered to. It can also document your attempts to communicate concerns to the district and their unresponsiveness or unwillingness to address them.

For instance, imagine your child's teacher started contacting you about his or her behavior problems in October. As the year went on, you heard numerous complaints, with no mention of possible solutions. It's now March, and positive behavior supports still haven't been put in place. When you receive a call from the principal informing you that your child has been suspended for fighting with another student, you're furious. You immediately contact your child's case manager to request an IEP Team meeting. You show up with your stack of emails from the past six months and ask to see the list of behavioral interventions the teacher has tried. Crickets . . .

Guess what just happened? Your paper trail helped to show that the school was not meeting all of your child's needs, nor their obligations under IDEA. They failed to evaluate your child in all areas of suspected disability and were getting ready to discipline your child for behavior that was likely a manifestation of his or her disability. You could easily file a complaint, but thankfully, it never gets to that point. Instead of suspending your child, the IEP Team decides to conduct a Functional Behavior Assessment (FBA) and put a Behavior Intervention Plan (BIP) in place. Your child's IEP is amended with this new information and the rest of the school year is smooth sailing. Pat yourself on the back, Mom. Well done.

Bottom line, an organized parent is a much stronger advocate. They're visibly more prepared and perceived more favorably. Compare this to a parent who rolls into an IEP meeting empty-handed and appears to be winging it. Which approach is more likely to keep your child's teachers, therapists, and case manager on their toes? I urge you to think carefully about the impression you want to make at the table and the role you want to play in your child's education. Take action accordingly.

The Homework Zone

I can't wrap up a chapter about organization without talking a little bit about everyone's favorite segment of the day—homework time!!!

The after-school hours can be a stressful time in most households. But for children who don't learn as effortlessly as their peers and their parents, even more so. Kiddos who have mustered every last ounce of energy to stay focused for six straight hours are physically and mentally exhausted by the time they walk through your front door. Tired manifests itself a little bit differently from person to person. Hyper, cranky, silly, and moody, are just a few of the fun possibilities. Add teenage hormones to the mix and you've got yourself a party! Hey, moms, doesn't sitting down with a long division worksheet at 4:00 p.m. sound like an awesome idea to you? I hope you can detect my sarcasm.

Maintaining an organized space for homework is going to be a lifesaver. You're going to have to do some planning ahead of time to make sure your child has everything they could possibly need within arm's reach. Index cards, graph paper, sharpened pencils, an extra set of textbooks, and a list of passwords to log in to school websites are just a few of the must-haves. The last thing you want to be doing is wasting time searching high and low for a glue stick or a pencil sharpener. Making the homework process as painless as possible is the goal here. Grab a portable table caddy from the dollar store and keep it stocked.

In my household, we have a strict after-school routine. My kids wash their hands, have a small snack, and then complete homework at the kitchen table before doing anything else. Once homework is done, they can relax with a preferred activity until it's time for dinner and sports.

For my learner who gets easily frustrated, it's not always that cut-and-dried though. If he's working with content that's particularly challenging, 10–15 minutes is about all we can manage in one sitting. Neuroscience tells us that the human brain can only handle one thing at a time. If the emotional brain is turned on, the thinking brain is turned off. There is absolutely no point in trying to push a child through an assignment once they're showing signs of frustration. Unless your adrenaline levels and blood pressure need a jolt, that is. More sarcasm, sorry! It's one of my survival tools when it comes to homework, and a much healthier alternative to shots of vodka and sleeves of Oreos. I digress . . .

But seriously, our children need us to remain extra calm when they're feeling anything but. I know this is easier said than done, but it's so important. When I see emotions starting to spill over with my son, I make him put his pencil down and take a short break. He might shoot a few hoops in the driveway, chew gum for some sensory input, practice deep breathing, take out the garbage, or listen to his favorite music. When he was younger, I'd have him jump on the trampoline, bear crawl around the house, or wrap himself up in his favorite blanket for a few minutes. Ideally, you're looking for enough of a break to reset and calm down, but not too long where it's impossible to get back on task. Experiment to see what works best for your family. Something visual, like a timer, can help if your child needs a concrete prompt to switch gears.

Communication about homework is super-important. When it starts to become a daily struggle in your home, please let your child's teacher know. You can write them a quick note at the top of each homework assignment that is particularly challenging. Include the amount of time spent on it too. Otherwise, the teacher has no idea about the exorcism (oops, I mean effort) that is taking place behind the scenes. They see the finished product that comes in the next morning but not the time, blood, sweat, and tears that went into producing it.

Don't forget to document your child's homework experiences and make it part of your own paper trail too. Grab your IEP notebook and jot down dates, assignments, time spent, and how much support your child needed. If you ever need to advocate for additional services, these observations can help provide the necessary evidence to make your case.

The purpose of daily homework is to PRACTICE the skills introduced in school. It's not to have parents teaching something brand-new. If your child is struggling with an assignment to the point of tears and frustration, it's not appropriate. And if he or she is showing signs of full-blown shutdown, then you need to contact the teacher ASAP. For something as urgent as this, I also recommend copying your child's case manager on the email to keep them in the loop.

You might want to discuss modified homework assignments and expectations with the IEP Team. An option I've seen work well for some families is timed sessions. Basically, the child is only required to spend a designated number of minutes per day on homework. The parent sets a timer and once it goes off, that's a wrap. Period. End of story. The parent draws a line on the worksheet or in the student agenda and the child is only graded on the work completed above the line.

An epic homework meltdown is really an attempt to communicate. In the most impassioned way possible, the child is asking for help. They need our patience and strength more than ever. I hear myself telling my kids the same things I used to tell my students when I saw them struggling in my classroom. I lighten their load by taking ownership of MY role. I explain that learning is a team effort. If they're not "getting" a concept, then their teacher and I need to do a better job of teaching it. Their only responsibility is to show up, stay positive, and try their best using the resources that have been provided. I reassure them that they're not alone. We're in this together.

CHAPTER 11
Keep Raising the Bar

My teacher thought I was smarter
than I was—so I was.
— **SIX-YEAR-OLD**

High expectations all around are a vital part of parent advocacy. I think I speak on behalf of most parents when I say that we already come to the table with high expectations for the team of professionals meeting with us. That's the easy part. In fact, I might go so far as to say some parents have expectations that are so high they're unrealistic. But that's what we do as parents. We want only the best for our kids. Especially for those of us who live in areas where property taxes are sky-high, we expect our schools to perform.

It's also important to examine the expectations we hold for our children, no matter what disability classification is typed onto page 1 of their IEP, or how high or how low their standardized test scores; no matter what the books, the doctors, or your mother-in-law's neighbor's cousin has to say about "kids like yours." You need to put all of that aside and stay laser-focused on your unique child. I can pretty much guarantee that your child is capable of more than you think. I know mine surprise me on the regular. Maintain expectations that are appropriately ambitious and watch them rise to meet them every time.

When you look in the mirror, are you holding yourself to the same standards of excellence? Be honest. Are you meeting the educators halfway? Have you committed the time and energy required to do your part? Parents, your role is critical. Are your expectations for your own performance high enough?

High Expectations for your Child

When the most recent version of IDEA was published in 2004, it highlighted the need for high expectations for special education students loud and clear. In the statute's very first section it states, "Almost 30 years of research and experience has demonstrated that the education of children with disabilities can be made more effective by . . . having high expectations for such children and ensuring their access to the general education curriculum in the regular classroom, to the maximum extent possible . . ." (20 U.S.C. § 1400(c)(5)(A)). This is a very powerful federal mandate, one that IEP Teams should be using to guide all decision-making. But who is going to hold them accountable for doing so? Grab a mirror—you're looking at 'em!

Critics of special education argue that students can get "stuck there," as if it were a large room with a floor made of quicksand. They caution that too many children with IEPs are labeled, removed from general education, and never return. Unfortunately, it's not such a far-fetched scenario. I've seen it happen firsthand.

You see, when a child is placed in a more restrictive setting, such as a self-contained classroom or a private school for children with disabilities, it's easy for teachers to lose sight of grade level expectations. They're stuck in their own little bubble of sorts. Without a consistent frame of reference, students run the risk of falling further and further behind their same-age peers. The impact of lowering the bar and leaving it there affects children exponentially. As parents, we need to make sure this doesn't happen.

The same concern can be voiced when it comes to over-modifying and over-accommodating. For example, does a student really need modified tests or a 1:1 aide year after year? Or can they eventually be taught how to be successful with less intensive support? Over time, students can become so overly depen-dent on an intervention that it hampers the natural development of the skills needed to compensate. It's a very slippery slope. The ultimate goal should always be to promote independence and transition students back to the general educa-tion setting as quickly as possible. Take a look at your child's IEP. Is it preparing him or her to achieve these goals?

I work with the family of a fifth-grader with significant behavioral chal-lenges. He attends a specialized day school equipped to meet his needs. Zach's mother wants him moved to a less restrictive setting, closer to home. Unfortu-nately, he has some aggressive and oppositional behaviors that are making that move unlikely for the time being. At our last IEP meeting, his case manager was thrilled to share that their behavioral data was trending in the right direc-tion. Instead of spending more than half of his day in the "cool-down room," Zach's time out of the classroom was now down to about 20 percent. He had been in two other placements with hardly any progress reported, so this was definitely cause for celebration. Finally, we had evidence that their behavioral interventions were working.

So then I asked what I thought was the next logical question: "What can we do to get that number down even lower?" The others gathered around the table just stared at me. You could hear a pin drop. Eventually, the lead therapist commented, "Given the child's diagnosis, we don't think that's very realistic." To which I wanted to say, *"Oh really? Then what the heck are we doing here?"*

But I bit my tongue instead and replied, "I don't expect it to happen over-night, but isn't returning Zach to his home school the larger goal that we're all working toward?" There was more uncomfortable silence, lots of paper rustling, and even one eye roll. And then, we began the process of leveling up his IEP and behavior plan.

Moms, we must, must, must keep raising the bar. Often, that's the single most important contribution we can make to the IEP process. If we don't main-tain the very highest expectations for our kiddos, why should anyone else? We cannot let complacency prevail over urgency on our watch.

Think about how our own behavior changes when a little additional urgency is introduced. Take the two hours before houseguests arrive for the holidays, for instance. I don't know about you, but I go into full-blown white-tornado mode. I can magically accomplish a zillion things in the span of a few hours. My kids and poor husband know to pick up their messes, take cover, and stay out of my path. Without fail, the finished product sparkles from top to bottom.

On a day-to-day basis though, do you attack the crumbs on the counter and toothpaste in the sink with the same intensity? I sure don't. The difference boils down to expectations. When we try to make our homes picture-perfect for entertaining, we've set the bar extremely high. Our motivation and behavior change to meet the demands of the challenge, and the finished product is magazine worthy. High expectations yield high performance. On your average weeknight though, most of us have much more relaxed standards. *Eh, that sink full of dishes can wait until I get back from soccer practice.* Or, *let me just scroll on Instagram for a few more minutes and then I'll put away the laundry.*

This same principle applies to teaching and learning. High expectations for student performance require increased action, effort, and intensity from not only themselves, but also, their teachers and parents. The result? Maximum student progress. Let me be clear though. I'm talking about expectations that are bold, yet still realistic. This part is crucial. Goals that are appropriately ambitious "in light of the child's circumstances," to borrow some of the language from relevant case law on the topic.

And guess what? Our kids want to be pushed. They want to be challenged. They want to be believed in. And they will thrive as a result. Think about the best teachers and coaches you've had in your life. I'm willing to bet that the first ones who come to mind are those who pushed you the hardest. Those who were firm but fair. Those who held the highest expectations for your growth and development. And guess what? You loved them for it! You respected them for it. Why? Because they inspired you to work harder than ever before. They pushed you past the limits of what you thought you could achieve on your own. And what happened to your self-confidence as a result? It soared.

There was an incredible home video that went viral on social media last year. A mother from Brazil was helping her 7-year-old son with cerebral palsy ride a skateboard. The boy suffered a stroke when he was just 20 months old, but had always dreamed of skateboarding. He couldn't walk independently, so how in the world would it ever happen? Enter a professional skateboarder who heard the story. His design team built a frame out of PVC piping that resembled a rolling phone booth. The boy was strapped safely into a harness, attached to a skateboard, and then his mother was able to push him up and down the ramps of a skatepark. Was it easy? Not at all. Did it take some creativity and courage? You bet. Was it worth it? Based on the size of the boy's smile, one million percent YES!

This story illustrates that truly ANYTHING is possible. For students with even the most complex educational needs, it's also possible to design the right framework to guide them anywhere they want to go. So, let's continue to have big dreams for our children. Let's only craft IEPs with the endgame in mind. And then let's approach each year, each week, and each day with the right amount of effort and urgency needed to make these dreams a reality.

High Expectations for Yourself

By picking up this book and getting this far, you've already proven yourself. You want to be the best advocate for your child that you can be, and you are ready to elevate your mindset and behavior in order to complete the mission. Because here is the truth. Your child gets only one ticket for this thrill ride called Life. There are no second chances. There are no do-overs. Your baby deserves the absolute best that you and everyone else in his or her life have to offer. It's that simple.

Now is not the time to be passive. Now is not the time to put all of your faith into a group of strangers who don't know your child like you do and who have dozens of other children vying for their attention too. The other members of the IEP Team are only human. Mistakes happen. Services get skipped. Timelines expire. Kids fall through the cracks. Symptoms of learning challenges are missed . . . especially if your child is hardworking and well-behaved. It doesn't mean that your child's teachers are incompetent or that your child's administrators are cold-hearted. On the contrary, these are educators you're dealing with. People who have dedicated their lives to helping children learn and grow. But, without a doubt, you should hold them accountable. In fact, it's your obligation to do so. Is this going to mean extra work for you? Definitely. Is it worth it? Absolutely. The pain of regret is a much, much heavier burden to bear.

Moms, stop being "too nice," and grant yourself full permission to advocate for your child. I know none of us want to be "that parent" who has a reputation for being demanding, impossible to please, or worst of all . . . crazy! But, pretty please, don't let that fear stop you from getting more involved with your child's education. Yes, you're going to need to take a more assertive stance, which might seem beyond your comfort zone. But advocacy doesn't have to be scary. There are plenty of actions you can take that are both savvy and completely benign at the same time. Let's start there.

Think about the many ways that you can offer a helping hand. Literally. Become a room parent or volunteer to help chaperone class trips. Sign up to help with the book fair or spirit week, or to make photocopies in the office once a month. Physically get yourself into your child's learning environment as much as possible. Not only will you feel good about yourself for donating your time, but you'll be establishing yourself as an ally, a teammate. As a bonus, the bird's-eye view of your child's learning environment and how they're responding to it will be invaluable.

You can also help by donating items to the classroom that your child will benefit from. For example, if he or she needs a quiet place to calm down, consider offering to send in bean bag chairs, fun pillows, or a small futon. If your student's IEP includes frequent breaks, think about what you can do to help out. Offer to send in a timer that's super-simple to operate or better yet, start teaching your child how to manage this accommodation themselves.

I once worked with a savvy mom who gifted her child a digital watch for his birthday. She taught him how to set an alarm to go off every hour as a reminder to take a short break. Instead of putting all of the responsibility on the teacher, who was busy running the entire classroom, she got creative and took the reins.

Her son learned some important self-monitoring and self-advocacy skills in the process, so I would definitely call it a win for everyone involved.

If there are particular fidget toys or sensory items that help your child self-regulate, offer to send them into school. If you think a pair of noise-canceling headphones would be a game-changer, purchase a pair on Amazon and send them in. Could you ask the school to provide all of these things? Most definitely. And I'm pretty certain they would, especially if listed as a need in the student's IEP. But if your goal is true home-school partnership, there's a great benefit to meeting them halfway when you can.

I once worked with a family whose fourth-grader was identified as a gifted learner. Unfortunately, there weren't many enrichment opportunities being offered by the teacher. Grace's love of learning was quickly replaced by boredom. With her innate curiosity fading fast, her parents started to worry. Even after meetings with the teacher and principal, numerous attempts at advocacy, and many sleepless nights, they didn't see much changing. And so, we decided to channel their energy in a more positive direction. They searched the internet for self-guided projects that Grace would both enjoy and feel challenged by. They sent them into school for her to work on when she was finished with her classwork. The teacher agreed to conference with Grace about them regularly and then allowed her to present her creations to the class.

In an ideal world, should a parent have to do all of this legwork? Well, no. I mean, isn't that a teacher's job? Well, yes. But the truth is that life isn't perfect. And neither is public school education. There are inherent limitations of money, time, highly skilled staffing, resources, etc. As parents, it's incumbent upon us to pick up the slack when necessary. It's up to us to help co-create the learning experience we want our children to have. Your child will be the ultimate beneficiary.

We have to be open to finding creative solutions to problems when they arise. If you want your child's experience at school to be the best it can be, get in the game. You can't sit on the sidelines and point fingers at the school system. Well you could, but that's not going to get you or your child anywhere. Instead, ask yourself: *Did I do my part? Was I as collaborative as I could be? Did I do every-*

thing that I could to advocate along the way? What else can I do to support my child's teacher? When everyone is working together at full capacity, the greatest outcomes will be achieved. Your child will go the farthest and the fastest and be the happiest. I can't think of a better definition of school success, can you?

Shift your mindset. Get involved. Raise the bar.

Ask all the questions. Offer suggestions. Think outside the box.

Don't accept the status quo. Push the envelope. Be the squeaky wheel.

As long as you do it respectfully. With a smile on your face and your hand extended.

This is savvy advocacy.

CHAPTER 12

Focus on FAPE

When parents first reach out to me, it's always for the same reason—they're concerned about the education their child is receiving. Either they are opposed to something already happening and want to make it stop, or they are frustrated by the school's inaction and want to know how to get them to do XYZ. Creating change isn't always easy though. Most of the time, parents have already tried to advocate for their child's needs, but their requests have been ignored or denied. They're tired of going in circles. They're fed up with feeling steamrolled, so they contact a professional advocate.

My approach is always the same too. After examining the student's records, I look to see if there is a legal basis for their requests. Is there an expectation specified within district policy, state special education code, or federal law that the school is not meeting? If I can find something, the parents will be able to make their case to the rest of the IEP Team so much more effectively. Sometimes even just using the right language, borrowed from one of these sources, has a powerful effect on their advocacy efforts.

And so, I want to give you a high-level overview of the school's legal obligations to you and your child. You might be pleasantly surprised to learn that it's a pretty meaty list. Remember, special education law was written with the rights of students and parents in mind. **Local education authorities (LEAs)**, the fancy name for public school districts, are expected to abide by them. When you boil all of the statutes, regulations, and case law out there down to their essence, public schools have two important responsibilities:

1) Provide your child with an appropriate education

2) Allow parents to participate fully in the process

Failure to do either or both is a violation of your family's rights. You're not going to let that happen on your watch, are you?

I believe that one of our roles as parents is to hold our LEAs accountable. To ensure that they're not merely following IEPs, but are also trying to move our children as far along in their educational journeys as possible. I have very high expectations for educators. I'm pretty certain that you do too, or you wouldn't be here. Warning—the content in this section is a little dry and contains more legal mumbo jumbo than you'd probably like. But, if learning this stuff is going to help your child receive what he or she needs, then it behooves you to grab a highlighter, get cozy, and jump on in!

The Rules of the Game

If you're looking to improve your advocacy game, it's time to get really familiar with the rule book. Start with your state's Special Education Code. It contains all of the guidelines that school districts must abide by in their provision of special education services. Everything is spelled out from the number of students allowed in each type of classroom, to evaluation timelines, to the steps a parent can take when they disagree. Each state code is derived directly from the IDEA, the federal law governing special education. State laws cannot provide less protections than the federal law, but can expand upon them, offering parents and children even more rights. The New Jersey code is 187 pages of rich advocacy goodness. My copy is a highlighted, sticky-noted, dog-eared and tattered mess at this point. Not a day goes by that I don't consult it for some reason.

In New Jersey, our State Department of Education has distilled the most relevant parts of its code down into a 49-page handbook aptly named Parental Rights in Special Education (PRISE). It's parent-friendly, organized into FAQ format, and features an appendix full of important terms, forms, and parent resources. I'm willing to bet that other states have something similar. You may have even been physically handed a copy at your last IEP meeting. See how easy they make it for us to become better advocates for our kiddos? Put this book down and go check to make sure that you have a hard copy on hand. If not, print one from your state's Department of Education website or request one from your child's case manager. This booklet should be your very first stop when you have an advocacy-related question. Most of the questions I hear from parents every day can be answered with the PRISE.

If you're looking to expand your understanding of special education law beyond the basics, you can find links to these primary sources on the US Department of Education website:

- Individuals with Disabilities Education Act (IDEA)
- Code of Federal Regulations (CFR)
- Section 504 of the Rehabilitation Act of 1973
- Americans with Disabilities Act of 1990 (ADA)
- US Department of Education guidance letters from the Office of Civil Rights (OCR) and the Office of Special Education Programs (OSEP)

These are the other two websites I send parents to when they wish to learn more about the interpretation and application of special education law:

- Council of Parent Attorneys and Advocates (COPAA)
- Wrightslaw Special Education Law and Advocacy

The Right to FAPE

In the United States, children with disabilities between the ages of 3 and 21 are guaranteed a free and appropriate public education (FAPE). It's a phrase that you have heard before, but what does it actually look like in real time? Well, the free, public, and education parts are pretty straightforward. The word *appropriate*, however, is what really matters. It's what the fidelity of the entire IEP hinges upon. There's one teeny, tiny problem though: *appropriate* is wide open to interpretation. It's extremely subjective. What is appropriate is different for every child.

Now, let's take an in-depth look at four of the most common ways to think about FAPE. If you're concerned that your child won't be fully prepared for life after graduation, isn't making measurable progress, doesn't have enough access to neurotypical peers, or isn't getting all of their educational needs met, then you have a major problem on your hands. You could argue that the IEP isn't doing what it's supposed to do; likewise, that the school district has failed to do its job. If you have concrete evidence to back up your concerns, each of these four scenarios could be the basis for the legal claim that your child was denied FAPE. In other words, that your child was denied one of his or her basic educational rights.

1) An *appropriate* education <u>prepares your child for life after graduation.</u>

What follows might be the most important line in the IDEA. To be honest, I can't think of a higher expectation that can be set for our public schools. Not only are children with disabilities guaranteed specialized instruction for each school year they are deemed eligible to receive services, but the ultimate goal is to "prepare them for further education, employment, and independent living" (20 U.S.C. § 1400(d)(1)(A)). A formal **transition plan** isn't created until the school year that a student turns 16, but each and every IEP should be written with a long-term vision in mind.

For example, imagine that your 17-year-old with Down syndrome hasn't received pre-vocational training this year because the district's job coach was out on maternity leave. Without this important hands-on instruction, you could argue that your child was denied an appropriate education. When you find yourself in a situation like this, put your concerns in writing and request an IEP meeting to discuss them. Your email might say: *"I'm very concerned that Taylor didn't have the chance to practice her job skills in the community this year. I'd like to request an IEP meeting as soon as possible to discuss her transition goals and how we're going to make up the lost instructional time.*" Then see what suggestions the team offers in order to make amends.

If a student with a disability is college-bound, it's essential that their course-work throughout elementary, middle, and high school is rigorous enough to prepare them for it. Pay attention to the course titles and curricula utilized whenever your child is pulled out of general education for instruction. A very bright ninth-grader I work with was placed in a Behavior Disability classroom for one year following a disciplinary infraction. There were many reasons why we felt it wasn't an appropriate environment, not the least of which was the loss of college prep level instruction. You see, all subjects were taught by the same special education teacher, as opposed to content area teachers with advanced training in the subject they teach. Instead of Algebra 1, the student would be enrolled in Math 9; and instead of College Prep Biology, the student would receive something called Integrated Science. We asserted that the quality of Anthony's education in the self-contained setting would be less than what his non-disabled peers were receiving. Further, that it would fail to set him up for academic success in the rest of high school and beyond. Anthony is a complex kid. A much more individualized program was necessary to meet his needs.

When a child is very young, it can be difficult for parents to imagine them as teenagers, let alone anything beyond that. School teams can lose sight of the future as well, since immediate attention is given to the curriculum standards for each grade level. Don't get me wrong, it is important to "zoom in" each year and meet your child where he or she is at that moment in time. But don't neglect to marry that with the larger vision that you hold. Make this the north star that you use to guide your advocacy efforts year after year.

2) An *appropriate* education <u>enables your child to make meaningful progress.</u>

The *Endrew F. v. Douglas County School District* (2017) case is arguably the most important decision about special education to be handed down from the

Supreme Court in recent years. It affirmed that the instruction children with disabilities receive must provide more than just a minimum educational benefit. Further, ". . . a student offered an educational program providing 'merely more than *de minimus*' progress from year to year can hardly be said to have been offered an education at all." In other words, IEPs should be "appropriately ambitious." This call for higher expectations is a major victory for our kids, as it really raises the bar for public schools across the US. It provides leverage for parents to demand that their child makes measurable progress each year.

For example, suppose your fifth-grader with dyslexia has been stuck on a second-grade reading level for two years. According to the running records taken by his teacher, Colby moved from a level J in October to a level K in May. She insists this is evidence that he is making progress. In your mind though, it's not enough. How in the world is he ever going to be a proficient reader at this rate? When you find yourself in a situation like this, put your concerns in writing and request an IEP meeting to discuss them. You can write, *"I'm concerned because Colby has hardly made any progress in reading this year. I'd like to request an IEP meeting to discuss whether additional services or a different intervention is required at this time."*

If you have solid evidence that your child has made little to no progress toward his or her IEP goals, and the school isn't actively working with you to rewrite the IEP, that should sound an alarm. In my opinion, you could argue that your child's educational program is not appropriate. We'll talk about this topic in even greater detail in chapter 19.

3) An *appropriate* education takes place in the least restrictive environment (LRE).

We already know that debates about appropriate placement are some of the most common and most heated at the IEP table. Heck, the topic of inclusion is even argued about among fellow special education parents on social media. Because there are so many unique factors at play, the conversation can get super complicated very quickly. At the end of the day though, every child has the right to be educated with their general education peers to the greatest extent possible.

For instance, what if you're worried that your third-grader with autism has picked up inappropriate behaviors from other students in her self-contained class? Olivia has recently started hitting and yelling at home, two things she has never done before. She struggles greatly with social language skills, but the only period of the day in which she is exposed to neurotypical peer models is lunch. And by the way, Olivia sits with her classmates and their aides at a separate table, having minimal interaction with anyone else. When you find yourself in a situation like this, put your concerns in writing and schedule an IEP meeting to discuss them. Your email to the case manager might ask, *"Can we please meet to talk about increasing opportunities for Olivia to learn alongside her peers? I'm concerned that not only is she picking up some bad habits from her classmates, but also that she isn't being included meaningfully. Olivia's father and I want her to be educated in the LRE to the greatest extent possible."* We'll talk even more about advocacy strategies regarding placement and inclusion in chapter 20.

4) An *appropriate* education <u>meets ALL of your child's needs.</u>

Some IEPs are rock-solid when it comes to meeting the majority of a child's needs, but fail to target others. The plan is incomplete, and thus, inappropriate. Anthony's case above is a perfect example. Remember, special education is responsible for the full educational performance of each child with a disability. It's not only about academics. Functional skills, such as appropriate behavior, life skills, and social skills, must also be addressed if necessary. Otherwise, it would be like putting a car out onto the road with only two or three tires instead of four. Even if those tires are made of the highest quality rubber and the rims are polished to perfection, the car isn't going to get very far.

For example, imagine that your first-grader with ADHD has an IEP that has helped him improve his attention in the classroom. Unfortunately, Ben keeps getting sent to the principal's office for misbehavior in the hallway, bathroom, and library. Also, he came home crying the other day because the other children on the playground run away when they see him coming. When you find yourself in a situation like this, put your concerns in writing and request an IEP meeting to discuss them. You can say: *"I'd like to request an IEP meeting to discuss Ben's impulsivity. I'm concerned that his current behavior plan isn't enough. He's doing great in Mrs. Smith's class, but is still struggling in other settings. Also, Ben is having a hard time finding friends to play with at recess, and he's very upset about it. I think it's related to his ADHD. Can we address social skills in his IEP?"* We'll dive much deeper into conversation about behavior management in chapter 21.

* * *

In serious situations like the four of these, if your attempts at advocacy are getting you nowhere, it's time to lawyer up. Please, please, please make sure you're putting all of your concerns and requests in writing along the way. Also, collect as much evidence and data as you can to document what is taking place.

I hope these examples clarified the alphabet soup of special education for you. FAPE, LRE, and IEP are the three acronyms that are most fundamental to your child's rights. They are likely to be at the heart of your advocacy efforts and are interrelated. To summarize, make sure you're holding educators accountable for providing a Free Appropriate Public Education in the Least Restrictive Environment via a well-written Individualized Education Plan. If you can work collaboratively to achieve all of that, everyone wins. Most importantly, your child.

CHAPTER 13
Know Your Rights and Assert Them as Needed

Do you feel like a FULL participant in the IEP process? An EQUAL member of the team? That your opinions and suggestions are VALUED? If you answered no to any of these questions, this chapter is for you. You might be surprised to learn that parents have a long list of rights that are specific to them. Parents have the right to be fully involved in every part of the IEP process if they want to be. If you're ever made to feel like an outsider, an afterthought, or a nuisance, it's very possible that your parental rights have been violated.

I've compiled a list of some of the most important federal procedures put in place for parents. The exact section of the IDEA or Code of Federal Regulations is included as a reference in case you want to learn more. You can even print out and take the relevant section of the law into your next meeting with you. Special education attorney Pete Wright is well-known for coaching parents to channel Miss Manners and Columbo, the clever detective from the '70s television show, for this purpose. The secret is to maintain a polite, non-confrontational stance while innocently asking the team to explain how a particular law applies to your situation. He has found this to be an effective way to both assert your rights and stay on good terms with the school district.

Rights Related to Evaluation and Eligibility

<u>Right #1</u>: **Parental consent is needed to evaluate, reevaluate, and classify.**

The school requires your consent prior to conducting the initial evaluation to determine if your child qualifies for special education. Likewise, they must obtain parental consent prior to any reevaluations. A parent's informed consent is also needed before special education and related services can begin. Essentially, the school district cannot formally assess your child, classify them, or implement an initial IEP without your full knowledge and written permission.

Legal Reference: 34 CFR § 300.300(a-c)

<u>Right #2</u>: **You have the right to review evaluation reports prior to an eligibility or IEP meeting.**

After a formal evaluation has been administered, a group of "qualified professionals," along with the parent(s), must have a meeting to review the results. The purpose is to determine whether the child has a disability, if they qualify for special education, and if so, what their educational needs are. Parents must receive copies of all evaluation reports prior to the meeting so they can be fully prepared to discuss them. They should never have to go into a meeting blind. If possible, I encourage parents to make a list of their questions about the evaluations ahead of time and email them to the team. This can help the meeting run even more efficiently. In New Jersey, evaluation reports must be provided to parents at least 10 days prior to an Eligibility Determination Meeting. Check your state regulations to see if a similar timeline applies.

Legal Reference: 34 CFR § 300.306(a)

<u>Right #3</u>: **You have the right to request an Independent Educational Evaluation (IEE).**

At any time, parents have the right to obtain an independent evaluation from an expert in the private sector and submit the report for consideration by the team. When a parent disagrees with an evaluation conducted by the school, they can ask for an "IEE at public expense." If granted, the district is expected to help arrange and pay for it. It's important to note that the school is not required to accept the results of an independent evaluation, nor implement any specific recommendations made, even if they pay for it. Their only obligation is to "consider" them. You can learn more about IEEs in chapter 20.

Legal Reference: 34 CFR § 300.502(b)(2)

Rights Related to IEP Meetings

<u>Right #4</u>: **You have the right to participate in IEP meetings.**

Parents are equal members of the IEP Team. But don't just take my word for it; it's explicitly stated in the IDEA. I know it doesn't always seem this way when you're sitting there like the odd man out, but it's critical that you understand your role. It's important that all of your questions are answered, all of your concerns are thoroughly discussed, and all of your suggestions are legitimately considered. Parents are entitled to request an IEP meeting at any time throughout the year. Also, there are no time restrictions on meeting length. If you're told that they need to "wrap it up so the teachers can get back to class," but not everything has been resolved to your satisfaction, you should request a continuation meeting.

Districts are required to take specific steps to encourage parent participation and attendance at meetings, and even keep a record of their efforts. Some examples listed in IDEA include: parents must be notified of meetings ahead of time, meetings must be scheduled at times that are mutually agreed upon, participation via conference call must be an available option, and interpreters must be made available if a parent is deaf or doesn't speak English fluently.

Legal Reference: 34 CFR § 300.322

<u>Right #5</u>: **You have the right to express your parental concerns.**

Did you know that there is a place in the IEP specifically dedicated to YOUR concerns as the parent? Unfortunately, I see it left blank way too often, even when a parent strongly disagrees with the plan that is outlined. IDEA explicitly states that the "IEP Team must consider the concerns of the parents for enhancing the education of their child." It's imperative that you voice your concerns at the IEP table, and make sure they are included in the document itself. When the IEP draft is submitted to you for review, if you're not in full agreement with how your concerns are presented, you can provide your own written statement and request that it be added.

Here's a great example to show how to use this particular parental right as an advocacy tool. If you believe that your child needs additional speech/language services, speak up and say that at the IEP meeting. Even if the rest of the team disagrees and determines that additional hours aren't needed at this time, at least there will be a record of your request in the parent concerns section. Three months down the road, when you see that your child isn't making progress toward his or her speech goals, you can point to your concern that is now part of the paper trail. Even though it took a few months, you now have a much stronger argument. With solid evidence to back you up, you are much more likely to get the increase in services you originally asked for.

Legal Reference: 34 CFR § 300.324

Right #6: You have the right to be involved in decisions about placement.

Once a student's needs, goals, and services have been determined, the final decision to be made at the IEP table is classroom placement. Where will your child receive his or her education? Does the appropriate setting exist in your home school? Do the programs in other schools in your district, or other local school districts, need to be considered? Parents must be actively included in this discussion. If the school district wants instruction delivered in a self-contained setting for the majority of the day, but you believe your child needs more exposure to his or her peers, say so. Give specific reasons why you feel the way you do. Similarly, if the other members of the IEP Team would like to place your child in the general education setting, but you're concerned about the pace of instruction and potential for frustration, speak up. Even better, ask to observe the continuum of placement options ahead of time so you are prepared to fully participate in the discussion.

Legal Reference: 34 CFR § 300.327

Right #7: You have the right to receive parent training.

Did you know that parent training can be one of the related services included in your child's IEP? If a parent requires counseling or instruction to assist in understanding the special needs of their child, it should be provided by the school district through the IEP. This might take the form of information about child development, or the teaching of specific skills or techniques. I've seen parent training provided for things like behavior modification and how to use augmentative communication devices. Bottom line, if you'd like additional guidance about your child's disability and how you can best support them in meeting their goals, ask for it. The frequency and duration of parent training sessions are listed directly in the IEP in the same way that other related services are.

Legal Reference: 34 CFR § 300.34(a)(8)

Procedural Safeguards

Right #8: You have the right to be notified about your procedural safeguards.

School districts are required to inform parents about their **procedural safeguards**, the requirements that exist to protect the rights of children with disabilities and their families, at least once a year. So, ignorance of the law is truly not a valid excuse when it comes to special education advocacy, Moms. In New Jersey, the information booklet created for parents is called the PRISE (Parental Rights in Special Education). I've also seen some districts hand out full copies of the State Special Education Code at each annual review meeting.

Legal Reference: 34 CFR § 300.504

Right #9: You have the right to receive written notice.

Thankfully, school districts cannot make major decisions about your child's education willy-nilly. They must always notify parents first in writing, whenever proposing or refusing to initiate or change the identification, evaluation, or educational placement of a child or the provision of FAPE to the child. This is referred to as **Prior Written Notice (PWN),** and is one of my absolute favorite advocacy tools to use.

When a parent makes a request and it is denied, you have a next move. Ask for written notice. Not only is the school district required to document the request that is being denied, but they also need to explain why. Written notice includes a list of the evidence/data utilized, a description of other options that were considered, and any other relevant factors that influenced their decision. So it's not as simple as a district saying, "Nope," and moving on.

To illustrate, if they're insisting that your child doesn't need the 1:1 aide you're asking for, the school needs to back up their viewpoint with an explanation and evidence. If they're saying that your dyslexic child doesn't require the highly structured multisensory reading program that you requested, they need to provide supporting documentation. If they're denying your nonverbal child the augmentative and alternative communication (AAC) device that her private speech therapist recommended, they must justify their decision in writing.

PWN ensures that parents are never left in the dark when it comes to what's happening with their child's education. Whether the district proposes a change at the annual IEP meeting or mid-year, written notification is always required. Be sure to look for it within the IEP or as a separate document.

Legal Reference: 34 CFR § 300.503

Right #10: **You have the right to utilize dispute resolution processes.**

My wish is that you and your child's educators agree about everything all the time. Sounds pretty amazing, doesn't it? Unfortunately, it's not very realistic. Differences of opinion along the way are inevitable. And sometimes, in spite of your best efforts to communicate, advocate, and negotiate a compromise that satisfies all parties, you're still not seeing eye to eye. So, now what?

IDEA offers parents several ways to resolve significant disputes:

1) You can file a **state complaint.**

A complaint is an allegation that an education agency (school district) has violated IDEA in some way. It can be filed regarding something that affected your specific child or a group of children, if the issue is more systemic in nature. Complaints are submitted to your state's Office of Special Education, which will conduct an investigation and make a determination. If the school district is found to be out of compliance, they will be given a corrective action plan. You can refer to your Procedural Safeguards booklet or your state's Department of Education website for more instructions and sample templates that you can use to file.

Legal Reference: 34 CFR § 300.152

2) You can request a **mediation conference.**

When you and your school district cannot agree upon an important aspect of your child's education, you have a decision to make. If it's not a hill worth dying on, you're better off relenting for the time being and requesting to reconvene in a few months to review progress. But, if the sticking point IS something that matters greatly to you, and you believe it will have a critical impact on your child, filing for mediation is an option to consider.

If both sides agree to participate, parents and school officials will sit down with an impartial third party in an attempt to reach a compromise. Basically, mediation is considered a kinder, gentler dispute resolution process compared to a due process hearing. Mediators are arranged through your state's Department of Education and free of charge. If it works, great! The mediator will draft a legally binding agreement on the spot, for all parties to sign. Even better, you just saved yourself the cost of an attorney, precious time, and the physical, emotional, and mental energy required to prepare for a court hearing and the appeals process.

Legal Reference: 20 U.S.C. §1415(e)

3) You can request a **due process hearing.**

If mediation fails, or if the school district doesn't agree to participate, you can file a due process complaint with your state's Department of Education. If you haven't been working with an attorney already, I strongly suggest that you hire one at this point. Prior to the hearing, both parties will be invited to attend a **resolution** session. This is a last-ditch effort to resolve the dispute without going to court. If an agreement isn't reached, the next step is a due process hearing, which is very similar to a trial. Both sides present evidence, call witnesses to testify, cross-examine them, and make legal arguments. In some states, the hearing officer presiding over a case is an administrative law judge.

Legal Reference: 20 U.S.C. §1415(f)

* * *

The savvy advocate in me considers complaints, mediation, and due process to be absolute last resorts. It's always in your child's best interest to develop a good working relationship with school officials, and use the skills and strategies I'm sharing in this book to resolve differences using the IEP process. Respectful communication, proactive involvement, and transparency will go a long way in this effort. When you take the formal dispute resolution route, you're taking a risk. It's possible that irrevocable harm may be done to the parent-school partnership. I'm not saying that there isn't a time or a place for legal action. It may be your only option. Please make sure that you consult with a professional advocate or attorney to carefully weigh the pros and cons before acting though.

Parents often cite fear of retaliation by the school district as a reason NOT to rock the boat. Sadly, there is a basis for this concern. I've seen administrators advise teachers to stop communicating altogether with "difficult" parents. While not very common, I have even heard of some calling truancy officers or filing false child abuse claims. I've spoken to parents who have felt bullied, intimidated, and in extreme cases, threatened. All of this is unacceptable, unethical, and may even be illegal. Section 504 of the Rehabilitation Act of 1973 specifically recognizes that those advocating for people with disabilities are protected from retaliation. If you feel like your family has been treated unfairly, you should contact the Office of Civil Rights (OCR) within the Department of Education for additional information.

I hope this chapter convinces you that yes, in fact, you do have an important voice in the conversation about your child's education. That it removes any and all doubts in your head about the power that parents hold. That your new knowledge allows you to walk away more emboldened to hold your school district to the highest standards. And that you realize that the law supports you and your child. Awareness is the first step. Once the lightbulb turns on, the real work begins. It's now time to take action.

PART 4

IEP Meeting Savvy

• • • ● ● ● ● • •

And now let me introduce you to one of the most anxiety-producing hours of the year . . . the IEP meeting. For most, it ranks right up there with dental cleanings and mammograms on the adult enjoyment scale. And the similarities don't stop there. All three have the potential to be awkward and leave you feeling exposed, vulnerable. No matter how much you dread going, alas, you know it's something you have to do.

Do you think walking into a meeting with your boss to review your job performance is hard? Try walking into a meeting with 5–10 "bosses" seated around the table, analyzing every nuance of your child's school performance. Where your child, an extension of you, is dissected under a spotlight for all to see. It can be rough, to put it mildly. But it doesn't have to be.

I hope that all of your IEP meetings are a complete breeze. That your child makes great progress year after year and that everyone walks out of the conference room with big smiles on their faces. But that isn't the IEP experience for all parents. There are some meetings that will push your emotional buttons. Some that are just plain heavy. And what's the common human response when one feels stressed? Fight or flight. I've seen it play out firsthand. Either a parent goes on offense and asserts themselves aggressively, or they shrink and get quiet as a means to escape. Remember from chapter 8 how the most effective advocacy style is somewhere in between those two extremes? In this part, I've gathered the best practices and tactics to help you achieve that delicate balance.

CHAPTER 14
Before the Meeting

Savvy advocacy is a year-round proposition—if you make it a priority to get involved, that is. Instead, I see too many parents of children with disabilities who view the Annual IEP Review Meeting as their singular opportunity to participate. It's my sincere desire to help change that.

I will admit that IEP meetings are where the magic happens though. There is nothing more powerful than the gathering of parents and professional educators on behalf of a child. Face-to-face communication is everything. It's the absolute best way to clear up the misunderstandings that are bound to happen from time to time. I've seen many parents walk out of the room feeling a whole lot lighter than when they walked in. I've even heard some breathe audible sighs of relief, reassured that everyone is back on the same page.

Once a year, the IEP Team convenes to review the child's progress toward IEP goals and develop a fresh plan for the following year. Parents can request an IEP Review Meeting at any time though. For more minor concerns, a parent-teacher conference would probably suffice. But if you'd like to discuss your child's education more broadly, getting the full team together is the way to go.

Prior to an IEP meeting, it's critically important that you take the time to prepare. Brady and Belichick never took the field without knowing their game plan inside and out. The duo was known for their hours and hours of preparation, and they have six, shiny Super Bowl rings to show for it. Since I want you to have the same level of success, here is your IEP meeting "pre-game" checklist.

☐ Invite people to attend with you.

Whatever you do, do not fly solo. Ideally, bring a spouse with you. When there are two parents at the table, actively involved in the conversation, it makes a huge difference. Forgive me for gender stereotyping, but I've observed with my own two eyes that when a dad speaks up at an IEP meeting, it's powerful. The team is less likely to issue a hard no, and they are more likely to be willing to problem-solve until all parties are satisfied. I can't really comment on why this is, but it makes logical sense that two educated, involved adults pack more of a punch than just one. If your partner cannot attend in person, I encourage you to have them participate via phone conference.

If nothing else, bring a close friend or family member who can provide moral support and take notes. There is going to be a lot of information shared, and it's going to be difficult to absorb and process it all on the spot. Per IDEA, parents are welcome to invite "other individuals who have knowledge or special expertise regarding the child" (20 U.S.C. §1414 (d)(1)(B)(vi)). So feel free to invite a professional who provides services to your child outside of school, such as a private tutor, therapist, coach, physician, etc. Really, anyone who can add meaningful input to the conversation. If an expert is unable to attend due to scheduling, ask if they'd be willing to write a statement for you. See if they can share insight they've gained from working with your child, and recommendations that might facilitate learning at school.

Make sure you inform the school in advance if you're bringing someone to the meeting. There should be a place to do this on the notice of the meeting that is mailed out to you. If you change your mind about who will be attending at the last minute, I recommend sending a simple courtesy email to the case manager to notify them.

☐   **Request a copy of the draft IEP.**

While some states have started to include it in their state code, there is nothing under federal law requiring school districts to provide parents with a draft IEP prior to an Annual Review Meeting. In fact, many of them eschew this practice because it suggests predetermination, which is a violation of your parental right to participation. The IEP is meant to be constructed in real time, with input from the entire team, including the parents. So, if a school comes to the table with 98 percent of it completed, it appears as if the parents didn't have much of a say in the process. I tend to look at a draft IEP as a necessary starting point though. It's a solid foundation to build upon. Realistically, if an IEP meeting started with a blank sheet of paper, the document would take hours and hours to create. Not very practical. Personally, I'd rather have my child's teacher teaching during those hours than sitting in a conference room with me.

If you've been told that you cannot have a draft in advance, and you've checked to make sure that the refusal is not in violation of your state code, request a copy of the "Present Levels of Academic Achievement and Functional Performance" instead. You may hear it referred to as "Present Levels," PLOPs, PLEPs, or PLAAFP for short. If you recall from chapter 7, this section of the IEP includes the most up-to-date assessment data, as well as your child's current strengths and areas of need as reported by their teachers. It's all gathered prior to the meeting, so there really isn't a basis for them to deny your request.

Knowing your child's Present Levels is valuable because it allows you to wrap your head around two things: 1) how much progress your child has made over the past year, and 2) which skills should be targeted in the new IEP. For instance, you can compare what's written in the Language Arts section of Present Levels to what was written in the IEP one year ago. How much reading and writing progress has your child made in that time? Did they achieve their Language Arts goals? If not, lack of progress should go to the top of your list of concerns to be discussed.

Reading the Present Levels section in advance of the meeting will also help you identify the areas of need requiring a corresponding goal and specialized instruction. For instance, if your son's kindergarten teacher reports that he ignores his peers when they try to talk to him, you can advocate for a social/emotional goal to foster friendship skills, or a speech/language goal to improve social communication skills.

When you're reading through the Present Levels, do so with a highlighter in hand. Every single time an area of need is identified, mark it, and add it to a master list that you're keeping. These are your targets for specialized instruction. When they hand you the draft IEP at the meeting, you can easily page through to make sure there is a corresponding goal to address each and every one. If there isn't, request that a goal be added.

Remember though, an IEP is the plan for what a child can reasonably be expected to achieve in one school year. Sometimes, certain skills and behaviors take priority over others and should be taught first. After thorough discussion, the IEP Team may decide to wait and address some areas of need in future IEPs and that's okay. Besides, the IEP is a living document. New goals can always be added mid-year if a student is making rapid progress and ready for more.

☐ Write a Parent Concerns letter.

This strategy works not only for IEP meetings, but any time you're meeting with a teacher. A few days prior, send an email to the case manager with a bulleted list of your biggest concerns and anything else you want to discuss. Ask that it be added to the agenda. Keep it short and sweet, and as always, maintain a professional, neutral tone, even if you're pretty darn angry about something. In addition to helping meetings run more efficiently, this technique serves several other purposes as well.

It gives teachers a chance to fully prepare for the meeting. They will be able to gather student work samples and other data that will be most meaningful in addressing your concerns. It also gives the team a heads-up so they can start problem-solving and thinking through the logistics of possible solutions in advance. This way, the conversation will feel less like a brainstorming session, in which solutions are proposed but nothing concrete is agreed upon. That's such a big time-waster!

Sending an email in advance prioritizes your parental concerns. There is nothing worse than frantically trying to squeeze in all of your questions in the last few minutes of a meeting, as teachers are gathering their things and preparing to head back to class. Does this sound familiar to anyone out there? Your meeting is scheduled for an hour. It starts 10 minutes late. The team takes turns describing your child's performance for the next 45 minutes, and then you're given the floor for the final 5. By that point, everyone's attention has already started to wander. Teachers are thinking about their next lesson. Others are glancing at the clock and thinking about the family sitting out in the waiting room. It's an all too common scenario. By making sure your concerns are added to the agenda ahead of time, you can avoid this rushed feeling completely.

Finally, it paints a positive picture of you as an involved parent; that you desire to be an equal partner in the education of your child. That you address concerns in a professional manner. That you are a parent who actually reads the IEP and quarterly progress reports. That you're likely to hold the school accountable for their role. All excellent qualities, if you ask me.

Here is an example of a simple Parent Concern letter:

Dear_____,

I look forward to meeting with you and the rest of the IEP Team on Thursday to discuss Emily and her progress in school this year. There are a few topics I want to make sure we have time to discuss. Please add the following to the agenda:

- Concern #1
- Concern #2
- Concern #3

Sincerely,

_____

Super straightforward, right? The Parent Concern letter is an easy advocacy tool to implement and can pay off big-time at the IEP table. More often than not, teachers are grateful for the advance notice, and come to the meeting fully prepared to problem-solve. Last school year, I attended a meeting where the case manager typed up an outline of the parent concerns, adding space between each one, and then handed out copies so everyone could take notes. It was one of the most productive meetings I have ever attended.

☐ Gather examples to illustrate your concerns.

Now that you've identified your biggest areas of concern and sent your email off to the meeting organizer, it's time to do exactly what the school is going to be doing . . . collect your evidence. This can take some time, so don't leave it until the very last second. By bringing concrete examples with you to the meeting, your concerns are more likely to be taken seriously. It's hard to dismiss or explain something away when it's an elephant in the room that's staring you right in the face.

When I say evidence, I'm referring to specific examples that support your concerns. It can be items sent home from school, like graded papers with teacher comments, work samples, progress reports, daily behavior sheets, standardized test scores, and report card grades. Perhaps even more compelling are the informal measures that you as a parent can gather. For example, work samples that your child has completed with a tutor, a homework observation log, and audio/video recordings that you've made of your child struggling through grade level material, among many others.

Let's suppose that you're concerned about your child's lack of progress in math this year. Sam's report card indicates that he's "progressing" and his teacher insists that he's doing "fine," but you're seeing meltdowns at the kitchen table every night. Through tears of frustration, he shouts things like, "I'm so dumb," and, "I hate math." It's heartbreaking to witness. You worry that Sam is getting moved along from grade to grade but he's not understanding the material. You're not sure what the solution is, but your gut is telling you that he's not getting what he needs. Maybe a different type of instruction would help? Or more hands-on materials? Or something else that you haven't thought of.

If you were my client, I would tell you to start a daily homework log to document exactly what's happening at home. First, record the amount of time math homework is taking each day. Next, jot down notes about any emotional outbursts or negative self-talk that occurs. Write down the exact words coming out of your child's mouth. And lastly, measure the amount of help needed to complete each assignment, on a scale from 1 (mostly independent) to 3 (needed extensive support). Boom! Now you have data to show that your child isn't learning and/or retaining the material being taught in school. By presenting your log at an IEP meeting and sharing the alarming statements your child has made, it lends credence to your concerns. The rest of the team will be much less likely to dismiss them as coming from a worrywart mom who is making a mountain out of a molehill.

Here are a few more creative ways to gather the type of evidence that can be useful at an IEP meeting.

Scenario #1:

You're concerned that your child has a reading disability and you'd like him evaluated for special education. DeSean has Bs and Cs on his report card. His teachers report that while they don't think he is a strong reader, he is holding his own in the classroom, so there is no evidence of a disability. *What can you do?*

Bring an audio recording of DeSean struggling greatly with a grade level text and play it at the meeting. Show them the homework log you've been keeping that lists the hours and hours spent each night, especially on subjects requiring the most reading. A private evaluation done by a reading specialist, along with their recommendations, would also be extremely powerful.

Scenario #2:

You're concerned that your child doesn't know how to make and keep friends, but social skills instruction isn't included in Carley's IEP. *What can you do?*

Jot down some real-life examples where you've seen her struggle socially. Is Carley a loner at the playground and birthday parties? Have you overheard her saying odd things to a peer? Does she reject other children's attempts to play? Record all of your observations in a notebook so you can easily share them at the meeting. If possible, request a classroom observation to see if you notice anything similar happening in school.

Scenario #3:

You're concerned that your son's self-injurious behaviors are increasing. Ben is now picking at his fingertips to the point that they are bleeding when he gets home each day. The school insists that they have the appropriate staff and program to meet all of his needs. *What can you do?*

Start documenting your concerns with daily photographs. Pictures of a child's self-inflicted injuries that are getting progressively worse over time are impossible to ignore. You can even take Ben to the pediatrician to report what is taking place and make sure there are no complications. Requesting to see the data collected by the classroom behaviorist is also recommended in this case.

All of the information gathered in these examples counts as data. And when it comes to effective advocacy in special education, data is king. The evidence that parents provide helps to paint a more complete picture for the team. It brings the whole child to life more vividly than test scores alone. Hard evidence makes the parents' point of view less subjective and so much more compelling.

☐ Be prepared to offer solutions.

Let me preface this section by stating that the educators sitting around the IEP table with you are the experts in their respective fields. They have the certifications hanging on their walls and the extra letters after their names to prove it. It's vital that you are respectful of this expertise. The occupational therapist should know more about fine motor development and sensory processing than anyone else there. The special education teacher should know the most about teaching interventions and multi-sensory strategies. And so on and so forth.

That being said, please, please, please don't underestimate YOUR ability to contribute meaningfully to the problem-solving portions of the conversation. Why? Because you also have an impressive list of credentials that started the moment your baby was first placed in your arms. You know more about your whole child and how he or she thinks/feels/behaves than any other human on the planet. You've been earning your parenting degree day in and day out for years, so don't shy away from proposing solutions that you think might be helpful. Just be mindful of your delivery.

When my son Kenny was struggling with following directions in fifth grade, the team and I were going in circles trying to identify the root of the problem. Was it an attention deficit? Receptive language issue? Anxiety? Auditory processing difficulty? Sensory overstimulation? His evaluations didn't yield any conclusive answers, so we were left scratching our heads, unsure how to proceed.

I thought about all of the seasons I'd spent watching him on the football field, basketball court, and wrestling mat. I noticed that other children picked up what the coaches were saying the first time, while Kenny struggled and seemed confused. But I knew that once the coach had his attention, repeated the instructions, and modeled the plays/moves directly, it would stick. For his particular learning style, new information needed to be presented as clearly and concretely as possible. Repeated practice was also part of his formula for success.

I shared my observations with the IEP Team, and they agreed to try similar methods in the classroom. I doubled down on the same strategies at home and we made sure that all of our expectations were aligned. Guess what? Kenny began to thrive. His feelings of overwhelm dissipated. Learning flowed much more easily. It didn't really matter what the root cause of his difficulties were anymore. Our focus shifted to helping him rise above them successfully. And he did.

Parents can also gather possible solutions through research and networking with other parents. Disability-specific websites and Facebook groups are excellent platforms to start learning about what other children with the same disability are having success with. Take note of the interventions and strategies that are recommended again and again and present them to the IEP Team. Think about asking questions like: "*Does the district have* this *program available?*", "*Are there any staff members familiar with* this *technique?*" and, "*Has anyone tried doing it* this *way before?*" Working together to flesh out the pros and cons of potential solutions is always a worthwhile exercise, in my opinion. Just remember that every child is unique. What works for one might not be a good fit for another.

Make no mistake about it. The experts at the table might not appreciate a parent with a degree from Google University acting like an authority. I've seen professionals get downright defensive when the slightest bit challenged. So, please tread lightly. It will be all about HOW you deliver the information and ask the questions. Think more "innocent suggestion" and less "know-it-all."

Their uneasiness makes perfect sense though, doesn't it? Imagine for a second that the roles were reversed and the team suggested that you start parenting differently. That you weren't doing things as well as you could and that they had some thoughts about how you could improve. I'm going to go out on a limb here and guess that it wouldn't go over very well! Personally, I would probably feel embarrassed, for starters. And then I could see those feelings transform into anger pretty quickly. *How dare they insult my ability to parent my own child, and in front of everyone no less! Are they serious right now?*

In the case of an educator, the internal dialogue might sound something like this: *Who does this parent think they are? They don't know what it's like to be a teacher. Do they really think I haven't tried that already? I know what I'm doing, thank you very much!* And guess what all of this emotion does to the parent-school relationship? Major damage. So please proceed with caution. Always remember to check your tone and body language regularly to make sure you're not pushing any psychological buttons unnecessarily when advocating.

* * *

Probably the most important advice I can offer to parents heading into an IEP meeting is to relax. If you've already completed the steps in this chapter, you're more than prepared and should feel very confident. Some parents put extra pressure on themselves because they think they have only this one shot to get it right. The truth is, the IEP is a living document. It can be amended at any time, and additional IEP meetings can be requested throughout the school year as needed.

Besides, what's the absolute worst thing that can happen?

You start to cry in the middle of the meeting? You definitely aren't the first, and won't be the last parent to do so. In fact, most conference rooms that I've been in have a box of tissues handy at all times. That's not a coincidence. While I don't recommend carrying on inconsolably, if a few tears are shed, it's perfectly fine. I've been there. It's okay, I promise.

You blank out and forget what you wanted to say? Not a problem. Ask for a short break to refer back to your notes and collect your thoughts.

You run out of time and don't get to ask all your questions or make all your points? Ask for a continuation meeting and actually schedule it before everyone leaves.

You make a request and the team replies with a big, fat NO? No worries! I've got you. I'll be sharing strategies for this exact scenario in Part 5.

A Few Final Tips . . .

- If you're not thrilled with the goals listed in the draft IEP, write your own and bring them to the meeting with you. There are a ton of sample goals on the internet, often sorted by grade level, academic area, and category of need.

- If you're going to be discussing your child's placement, ask for a tour of the in-district and out-of-district options prior to the meeting.

- If it's a meeting to go over evaluations that were conducted, make sure you have received all of the reports in advance. Read over everything carefully and make a list of the questions you have for the evaluators.

- Request a translator if your native language is something other than English. The school must provide one. You want to make sure there are no barriers preventing you from participating in the meeting fully.

- Let the district know if you're planning to record and if you're bringing anyone with you. Some states include a place for both on the form used to RSVP to the meeting.

CHAPTER 15
During the Meeting

....

IEP Meeting Day has arrived.

If you've read chapter 14 and taken action on the suggestions there, you're in great shape. Walking in with confidence is more important than you might think. It impacts your body language and the energy you give off, which can impact how your requests are received and how effective you are at communicating. So, lift that chin up, relax those shoulders, and plant a smile on your face. You can do hard things!

But if you're like many parents, the dialogue in your head doesn't sound very confident. Instead, you might find yourself bombarded by self-limiting beliefs like: *I'm not an expert. I have no idea what to ask for. I'm going to be so outnumbered. My ideas are going to get shot down, like always.* The problem is that self-doubt can threaten to sabotage your advocacy efforts. Do not let that happen. Get your mind right before you step foot in the door.

But, let's keep it real; IEP meetings can be profoundly uncomfortable at times. I mean for starters, nothing screams *awkward* quite like walking into a crowded conference room with a group of people sitting there, watching your every move. It reminds me of walking into church after the opening hymn. Or into a theater after the show has already begun. You can feel dozens of eyes on you, scanning up and down, judging. It's a blast! Okay, so maybe this portrayal is a teeny, tiny bit dramatic. But I don't know many people who can roll into these things completely at ease.

Nine times out of ten, the rest of the IEP Team is already seated comfortably, poised and ready to go. Their laptops are carefully laid out and their coffee is in hand. It's probable (although not necessarily in compliance with state and federal guidelines) that they may have even had a brief "pre-meeting" where staff members shared impressions and compared notes about your child. Their ducks are in a row and everyone is on the same page, ready to present a united front. Meanwhile, you're entering stage left, juggling your jacket and paperwork, turning your phone off, and making a sad attempt at small talk. You're not privy to the information discussed prior to your arrival, so you're already at a disadvantage.

The one and only thing that you have complete control over is your mindset. So, moms, it's time to flip the script. YOU are the real MVP for supporting the student on the home front. You are their first and most important teacher. You're the one making sure the articulation exercises, nightly reading, and science fair projects get done on time; that your student comes to school prepared to learn. And let's not forget that you're also the one teaching all of those valuable life lessons about friendship, effort, responsibility, and resilience. Maybe, just maybe, you're the last one in because you earned the right to make a grand entrance.

If I had a say in the matter, the rest of the team would rise to their feet and welcome parents with cheers and confetti. I have yet to hear of that happening though, so don't hold your breath! BUT, you can walk in with that mentality. That swagger. Confident in your belief about your role and your voice. Even though the classroom is technically not your domain, you are much more than just a guest at the table. You are an equal member of the IEP Team. Don't forget it.

Here are a few best practices to help you slay your IEP meeting game.

☐ Set the proper tone.

First things first. Let's start with some logistical matters. Always arrive on time. It's possible that the team may be running late, but you never want to make them wait on you. The teachers in attendance are taking time away from their students (your child included), so please be mindful of that. There is no dress code for IEP meetings, but I recommend business casual. You don't have to wear a suit and heels, but you should look put together and professional. An IEP meeting is like a business meeting. As a group, you're all going to roll up your sleeves and work TOGETHER to create your child's new IEP.

What to Bring

Never go into a meeting empty-handed. At the very minimum, you're going to need a notebook and something to write with. Make sure you bring your child's IEP binder if you have one, and any recent information the school has provided about your child. Specifically, your child's current IEP, the new draft IEP, report cards, progress reports, and evaluation reports. Beyond that, bring anything else that is going to aid you in your advocacy efforts. If you're going to record the meeting, have your smartphone ready to go.

Some parents like bringing a gift for the IEP Team, such as muffins, fruit, coffee, or flowers. This is definitely not necessary or expected, and some might even go so far as to argue that it's inappropriate. But, you have probably figured out by now that I'm a big fan of gratitude. And who better to show your appreciation to than the individuals who are spending six-plus hours with your child every day? Most of them are putting in time and energy above and beyond what is expected and doing about 20 extra things that aren't officially written into your child's IEP. They don't do it for the recognition, but simply because they're good teachers who care deeply about their students. Personally, I prefer giving small gifts with hand-written notes at the holidays and at the end of the school year. But, if your IEP Team is doing an exceptionally stellar job, and you feel called to take a plate of cookies to the meeting with you, go for it!

Lead with Positivity

Whether you bring something tangible or not, please make it a point to start the meeting in a positive way. Offer specific, genuine praise. Identify at least one thing the school team is doing well, and say thank you. This lays the groundwork for additional collaboration and productive communication. Yes, it's their job, but thank the team anyway for taking the time out of their busy schedules, away from their students, to meet with you. Thank them in advance for making you feel like a valued member of the team. Look everyone in the eye and smile. I know all of this sounds incredibly basic, but the impact of advocacy "soft skills" like these cannot be overstated.

Incorporate your Child into the Meeting

I think it's important to try to humanize the IEP process as much as possible. Parents can be the ones to remind everyone that an IEP isn't just a stack of paper stapled together. Rather, it's a fluid document attempting to capture the magnificence of a living, breathing child. The classification category listed on page 1 barely scratches the surface of your child's depths.

Beginning in the middle school years, it's customary to invite the student to attend their own meetings. Even before that, when parents feel the time is right, they should start talking to their children about their learning style, what's written in their IEP, and the accommodations and modifications they're entitled to. The sooner a student learns to self-advocate, the better. When I was an eighth-grade teacher, we would often have the bulk of the IEP meeting, and then bring the student in for the final fifteen minutes or so. We discussed the teacher recommendations for high school and asked for their input. If you think it would be a meaningful experience for your child to participate at an even earlier age, by all means, ask that they be included.

If your child is in preschool or elementary school, you can still find ways to incorporate them into the meeting. It's going to take a little more creativity on your part though. You can bring a framed picture of your child and prop it up right in the middle of the table. You can create a "brag sheet" or a "positive student profile" to share your child's interests and strengths, passing copies out to everyone on the IEP Team. There are dozens of excellent examples and templates out there on the internet.

Another option that I love, no matter what your child's age, is a written or video interview. Basically, you want to try to capture how school is going in his or her own words, and share it with the team. Here are the types of questions you can ask, but definitely tweak based on your child's age, ability level, and your biggest areas of concern: *What was your favorite moment from the school year? How would you describe yourself as a student? What are you really good at? What about school is the most challenging for you? What can your teachers do to help you learn? What are you most looking forward to in the upcoming school year? Is there anything that makes you anxious? What do you want your teachers to know about you? Can you describe your perfect learning environment?*

If your kiddo is on the shy side and doesn't want to be videotaped, simply interview them ahead of time and write down their responses. Some students may even prefer to write a letter or do a journal entry. You could ask them to free-write about their feelings and experiences related to school and see what they come up with.

I witnessed the power of this particular strategy firsthand while working with the family of an eighth-grade student with dyslexia. The IEP Team was recommending that Max be declassified at the end of the school year since, by all accounts, he was excelling. He was getting As and Bs, taking Honors Math, and was just named the student athlete all-star of the month. His parents were very nervous about the removal of services though, especially with such a big transition to high school coming up. They came prepared to the meeting with a letter that the child wrote, expressing how hard he was working in school and the many hours he spent each night on homework. Max described how much he benefited from being in a classroom with two teachers, because "one always knew how to explain things in a way that I could understand." He also shared how much his self-confidence had been affected by years and years of struggling to read. In his words, he has always felt "different and not smart" compared to his friends.

The teachers at the meeting were absolutely flabbergasted. You could see surprise and sadness on their faces as they listened to Max's mother read his words. He was a leader in the classroom, extremely popular, hardworking, and had a great sense of humor. He always presented himself as confident. After hearing the letter though, they realized there was so much more going on beneath the surface. They saw Max's stellar homework record and high test scores, but they didn't see the additional study time, tutors, and tears that went into achieving them. If this story doesn't hammer home the point that our children's needs are based on so much more than test scores and data points, I don't know what does. The team unanimously agreed to keep Max's IEP in place for the following year.

☐ Document the meeting.

As far as IEP meetings go, there's going to be A TON of information shared. The phrase "drinking from a fire hose" comes to mind. Parents often mention that they're not able to participate thoughtfully because they're too busy scribbling down what the teachers are saying. I suggest bringing a family member or close friend to serve as your note-taker while you listen carefully and advocate. Having an additional person by your side can also be extremely comforting, so do consider it.

To record or not to record? That is the question. There are some advocates who advise recording every meeting, every time. In my experience, placing a recorder on the table puts all parties on edge, making them less likely to communicate freely though. It changes the temperature in the room, so to speak. A parent runs the risk of sending the wrong message to the rest of the team. For example, A. That you don't trust them for some reason; B. That you're concerned they might say or do something improper; or C. That you're trying to "catch" them. But, if there is history of the school team promising things and not following through, or if you believe that the school district is violating any of the laws governing special education, then I absolutely recommend recording.

If you want to diffuse the tension surrounding recording, simply explain that it's something you do as a matter of course. It's part of your routine. You can say, "I have a really difficult time listening and taking notes at the same time. I record all meetings to make sure I don't miss anything." A short disclaimer like this makes the act of placing a recording device on the table seem less threatening.

Check to see what your state regulations and school district policy say about recording meetings. I recommend full transparency and notifying the school ahead of time if you plan to record. If there isn't a place to do this on the meeting RSVP form, a simple email to your child's case manager a day or two prior to the meeting will suffice. When you record, the district almost always chooses to record on their own device as well. This is standard practice, so don't be surprised when it happens. There are several easy-to-use apps out there for recording right on your smartphone. After the meeting, you can download the file, email it to yourself, and then save it for your records. A no-frills tape recording device can also be purchased on Amazon relatively cheaply.

If it's your child's annual review, and the district did not provide you with a copy of the draft IEP in advance, make sure you request one at the very beginning of the meeting. As the team goes through each section, follow along carefully and take notes in the margins as needed. Do not be shy. Ask questions, make suggestions, and get involved. If you prefer to be your own note-taker, don't stress about writing down every single thing you hear. Much of what will be shared about your child's current performance should already be captured in the Present Levels section.

At the start of your special education journey, create an IEP notebook where you document every meeting you have with your child's teachers and related service providers. Whether it's a phone call, a parent-teacher conference, or a formal IEP meeting, it's important to capture the main points that were discussed. This way, all direct communication is in one place and you're going to be able to stay organized more easily. Each time, start a fresh page and write the date at the top. Develop your own shorthand, using abbreviations and bullet points to save time.

☐ Create a Quick Sheet.

There is nothing worse than driving home from an IEP meeting and remembering something important that you forgot to ask. With information overload coming at you from all directions, and questions popping in your head like popcorn, it's highly likely that at least one of them will go unasked. To prevent this from happening and to keep yourself laser-focused, you need what I like to call a Quick Sheet.

A Quick Sheet is a single piece of paper that you use at meetings to record two important categories of information: *Questions* and *Outcomes*. You can fold a sheet of paper in half, labeling each section. The top half will be the place designated for your questions that come up during the meeting. The bottom half will be a place for you to list the agreed upon outcomes, and anything that needs to be followed through on. You can think of it like a post-IEP meeting to-do list. If your brain prefers to organize information vertically, side-by-side columns will work just fine too.

The *Questions* section is pretty self-explanatory. In addition to the list of your most pressing questions created ahead of time, you can quickly add the new ones that come to mind. Let's spend some time talking about what I mean by *Outcomes*, though. These are the agreements that the IEP Team makes. For example, if your child's speech sessions will be reduced from three times a week to two, write it down. If your child will have access to a new type of assistive technology to help with written expression, write it down. If your child will have 1:1 aide support in Gym class starting next week, write it down. All IEP changes should be formally communicated to you through a Written Notice form or the draft IEP handed to you at the end of the meeting; but it's important that you have your own list to make sure that everything matches up.

Even when a consensus is reached among team members, there may still be some loose ends left dangling in the breeze. These are items that require intentional follow through, or they run the risk of never happening.

Some examples of what I'm referring to:

- You agree to contact your child's doctor about sending updated medical records to school.
- The case manager is going to consult with the guidance counselor and then add another social/emotional goal to the IEP.
- Your child's teacher will start sending home extra math practice sheets on Fridays.
- The speech therapist promises to email you a list of social skills groups in the area.

It's important that you record all of these to-dos under Outcomes so you can make sure they get accomplished. There is a vast amount of ground covered at most IEP meetings. If you don't make a conscious effort to stay organized, something will inevitably get lost in the shuffle. Not because anyone is trying to get out of their responsibilities, but simply because educators and parents are ultra-busy and ultrahuman.

If you don't want to use a separate sheet of paper for your Quick Sheet, try this system using the same notebook that you're taking notes in. In the margin across the top, jot down all of your questions. In the margin on the left-hand side of the page, keep track of the outcomes. Whatever method you use, do not let the meeting end without looking back at both lists. Take the time to ask any questions that remain, and to read back all of the outcomes as you understand them.

☐ Speak up.

Now isn't the time to be a polite people-pleaser; to smile and nod, bobble-head-style. Now isn't the time to bite your tongue when you have a burning question right on the tip of it. Advocacy is never a passive endeavor. On the contrary, it's going to require courageous action on your part. Now is not the time to be shy.

One of my biggest IEP meeting pet peeves is when a case manager announces right off the bat that they only have 45 minutes since there is another meeting scheduled right afterwards. I've actually heard this exact statement before my bottom even hit the chair, more times than I'd like to admit. There is absolutely NOTHING about time limits for meetings in IDEA or any state regulations that I'm aware of. In fact, one could argue that imposing a time limit could lead to a denial of parental participation rights.

If the school team attempts to wrap up a meeting but there are still issues left unresolved and items that you want to discuss, politely ask to reconvene the meeting at a later time. Actually take out your calendar and schedule the follow-up meeting right then and there. You should never walk away from an IEP meeting feeling short-changed or rushed. Put on your advocacy hat and be assertive.

☐ Say THIS to get what you want.

Speaking the same language as your school team helps to level the playing field. It sends the message that you're more knowledgeable and prepared than the average parent. It indicates that you have high expectations for the school district to provide your child with a free and appropriate public education (FAPE). There are a few key words and phrases that I like to keep in my back pocket at all times. Some of the language is gently borrowed from federal and state law or case law, so it's powerful and commands attention.

First off, make sure that you replace the word *best* with the word *appropriate*. As discussed in chapter 5, your public school district is not required to give your child a "Ferrari" of an education, with all of the high-end bells and whistles. Rather, the magic word is *appropriate*. Legally, it's their responsibility to provide an appropriate education. So, instead of saying, "I want my child to be educated in the general education setting because it's the best environment for her," try this instead: "I want my child in the general education setting because it is the *most appropriate environment to meet her needs.*" Do you hear the difference? You've shifted the focus from what YOU WANT, to what your CHILD NEEDS. This is a critical distinction. As always, you should be prepared to provide solid reasons and examples that support your request.

I've gathered a few more examples of the type of language you will need at the ready. They can be applied to some of the most common scenarios that you are likely to encounter at the IEP table. Just tweak as needed and advocate away. I found the third set of dialogue on the *Center for Parent Information & Resources* website, an outstanding resource hub for parents.

Notice that I often use the word *we* when asking questions and trying to problem-solve. Especially if negotiations have reached a standstill or it's clear that team members aren't seeing eye to eye. This is the spirit of collaboration that is so fundamentally important to the IEP process. I'm intentionally trying to bring everyone back to a place of working together toward a common goal. My goal is to dissolve any "us versus them" tension that exists in order to create a mutually agreed upon IEP. I also want to send the message that unilateral decision-making is not okay. There is no such thing as one member of the team having the "final say."

Language to Use When Seeking Clarification

"Can you give me an example of that?"

"What strategies have you already tried to help Sarah with that?"

"Can I see the data to show that Sarah is making progress toward her goals?"

"What accommodations have been the most helpful, in your opinion?"

"I'm sorry, I'm not understanding what you're trying to say. Can you try explaining it in a different way?"

Language to Use When Stating Your Concerns and Seeking Solutions

"I'm concerned that all of Sarah's educational needs aren't being met. What else can we do to create an appropriate IEP?"

"I don't feel like this is the appropriate setting for Sarah. What other learning environments can we consider?"

"I'm concerned that Sarah isn't making meaningful progress. What other interventions can we try?"

"From what I'm hearing, Sarah's teacher could use additional resources and support. How can the IEP Team offer more assistance?"

Language to Use When Negotiations are at a Standstill

"We can all agree that this is not an easy issue. But we need to find a solution that will work for Sarah that we can all live with."

"I just don't see this as being appropriate for Sarah. There have to be other options we haven't looked at."

"I understand that you can't say yes to this request. Can you tell me who does have the authority? How do we get that person here?"

"Why don't we try this for six weeks and see how it works?"

"What will it take for us to reach an agreement on this issue?"

Language to Use When You Hear "No" or "We don't do that here."

"Can you show me a copy of the policy or law that states that?"

"Please document my concerns about this issue in the Parent Input section of the IEP."

"Please provide prior written notice that explains your position on this issue and why you're denying my request."

☐   Add your Parent Concerns to the IEP.

In chapter 13, we talked about your right to "meaningful participation" in the IEP process. Using the Parent Concerns section strategically is one of the most powerful ways to exercise this right. Leaving it blank would be a major missed opportunity. Before the meeting wraps up, ask how your concerns will be documented. Sometimes the staff member in charge will add a short summary on your behalf based on their notes. Alternatively, you can submit a statement in your own words and request that it be added.

I find that the Concerns of the Parent section comes in handy the most when the team can't reach an agreement about something. In the spirit of compromise, a parent may decide to trial the team's recommendations for several weeks, and then reconvene to review the results. For example, if you're advocating for your daughter to have a 1:1 aide for the following school year, but everyone else at the table insists that a shared classroom aide will be sufficient, what now? Instead of walking away feeling defeated or filing a formal complaint, you have another move. You can consent to starting the school year off without the personal aide, but ask that your child's progress be carefully monitored and measured. Let them know that you will be requesting an IEP Review Meeting 6 weeks into the year to look at the data and discuss how things are going. Ask that your concerns about a classroom aide and your intention to meet again in October be documented in the Parent Concerns section. Boom!

There's a good chance your child will be thriving in her new environment and that your school team was right. But, if the data shows that your child is struggling academically or behaviorally, your case for individual support has been made. Yes, it would have been wonderful to have what she needed in place on the first day of school. But now you're in a position to get her the next-best thing, an aide for the remainder of the school year. Effective advocacy doesn't always mean getting what you want the first time. Often, it's much more of a process. And that's perfectly okay.

A Few Final Tips . . .

- If at all possible, do not bring your other children with you. It will be a big distraction, and you won't be able to stay focused on doing the job of advocacy. Find childcare—trust me!
- Do not proceed with the meeting unless all IEP Team members are present. Nothing irritates me more than when parents are asked to

excuse someone because "they are teaching and there isn't any coverage." I'm a realist. I fully understand that it's not always convenient to gather all parties during the school day. I also realize that emergencies can arise. But it's terribly unfair to put parents on the spot like that and pressure them to acquiesce, especially if they had to rearrange their schedule and take time off work to be there. The members of the IEP Team are specified in the IDEA for a reason. Each one is important. Don't feel bad about insisting that the meeting be rescheduled for a time when the full IEP Team is in attendance.

- Request a 5-minute break if you need to, especially if emotions start to bubble up. Step outside into the hallway or take a quick walk to your car for some fresh air and a change of scenery.

- Never sign the IEP at the meeting. Technically, the only IEP that needs a parent signature at all is the initial IEP. All other IEPs after that will automatically go into effect after a certain number of days, even without your signature, unless you express your disagreement in writing. In New Jersey, the timeline is 15 days, but check your state regulations. Heads up though—you may be asked to sign an attendance sheet, and possibly another document to acknowledge you were given a copy of the Parental Rights packet or state code. This is standard practice.

- Be mindful of your body language and nonverbal communication, especially if you're the expressive type. Eye rolls, audible "huffs," and glaring are among the behaviors that should be avoided at all times.

CHAPTER 16
After the Meeting

After your child's Annual Review IEP Meeting, you may be very tempted to treat yourself to a mani-pedi on the way home to celebrate another school year down. And celebrate you should, but there is still some work to do.

In chapter 14, you read about how critical your preparation prior to a meeting is. I would argue that what you do AFTER the meeting is equally important. You can't just assume that everything that was discussed is going to be executed to perfection. Some things will slip through the cracks. Others will fall to the bottom of a busy teacher's priority list. The absolute best remedy to prevent this from happening is summed up with two simple words: *Follow up.* And then you're going to follow up some more. And then basically, you're going to keep following up for the rest of your child's school career. I'm not exaggerating, so it behooves you to develop some best practices and routines to help along the way.

Whether you're following up after an annual review or any other type of IEP meeting, your goals are the same. First, you want to document the meeting by putting the most important discussion points and outcomes in writing. Next, you want to communicate your takeaways back to the school district to make sure that everyone is on the same page. After that, your job will become all about accountability.

If you were given a copy of the draft IEP at the end of the meeting, or if it's sent home in your child's backpack later that day, your first order of business is to read it carefully from start to finish. Warning—it's going to be tedious and feel like a chore, but believe me when I say that it will be time well spent. I find errors in IEPs all the time. If you've ever found another child's name randomly sprinkled into your child's IEP, you know exactly what I'm talking about! Most mistakes are due to human error and are relatively minor. Others are much more significant and should be corrected immediately.

Here are a few questions to guide you:

- Are ALL of your concerns documented in the Parent Concerns section?
- Are all special education and related services listed, along with the correct frequency and duration?
- Is there a goal written for EVERY need that was identified?
- Are the goals specific enough, clearly written, and measurable?
- Are ALL of the modifications and accommodations that your child needs listed?
- Is every piece of technology that your child needs included?

Highlight any inconsistencies between what you recall from the meeting and what's written. Then make a list of the questions you have. Unless it's an initial IEP, most states have a specified number of days for you to review the IEP before it automatically goes into effect as written. Be mindful of this timeline but at the same time, remember that an IEP is a living, breathing document. It can be amended at any time throughout the year, and even during the summer months. Yes, the Special Education department in your school district is open all year long. Timelines are still in effect over the summer.

Send a Follow-Up Email

Next, I want you to sit down and prepare to write a thorough follow-up email. Basically, you want to document all of the pertinent information that was shared and everything that was promised to your child. Everything that was verbally agreed upon and every point of disagreement. Ideally, if the draft IEP is done well, much of this information will be included somewhere in the document.

But not everything will be. This is your chance to hammer home those points and "get it in writing."

Generally speaking, all of your follow-up emails will be structured the same way. Here is my five-paragraph formula:

1) **"Thank you so much for meeting with me today."** Always open with a line or two of gratitude. The more specific and genuine the better.

2) **"I reviewed the draft IEP and have these questions/concerns:"** List any errors that you discovered and/or wording that needs to be clarified, using bullet points.

3) **"As I recall, we also discussed the following:"** In this section you will summarize anything significant that hasn't been well documented in the IEP, in bullet point format. You can use your recording or meeting notes as a guide.

4) **"These are the outcomes that still require follow-up:"** This is where you will repeat the to-do list you went over at the end of the meeting. Include the agreed upon action steps, as well as the person responsible for each. Your Quick Sheet is really going to come in handy for this part.

5) **"Please let me know if I missed or misunderstood anything."** Invite the rest of the team to agree or disagree with your recollections.

I recommend sending your follow-up email to your child's case manager and copying everyone else who was in attendance. You want to make sure all parties are on the same page, and this letter can help you achieve that clarity. Most of the time, the team thanks me for providing such a thorough summary, and they agree that it's an accurate representation. They answer my questions and make minor changes to the IEP as requested. This is your chance to hold the team (and yourself) accountable for following through with everything that was promised. As with all other correspondences, this letter should have a polite and professional tone.

Beyond the IEP Meeting

I spend my days advocating for children to get the services they need in school. I am passionate in my belief that ALL children are entitled to an appropriate education. I don't believe that the full burden of responsibility to educate children lies squarely on the district's shoulders, however. Yes, the local school district takes the lead for approximately 6 hours a day, 180 days of the year, and a well-written IEP is one of their roadmaps. But then it's up to parents to step up during the after-school, weekend, and summertime hours when school is not in session.

The job of cultivating decent, educated humans is a shared responsibility. It truly does take a village. The best outcomes for kids are achieved when parents and schools take an equally active role. So, at the risk of sounding preachy, after the IEP meeting, please do your part. Most importantly, follow through on everything you said you would. You know that you're going to be holding the school team accountable in the weeks and months ahead, so doesn't it make sense to hold yourself to that same high standard?

Make sure your child has a predictable after-school routine and a quiet place to do homework. For moms of middle and high school students, the best advice I have is to be proactive. Regularly check your child's grades online. Start asking questions if you see a pattern of missed assignments or scores that are lower than expected. Talk to your child and coach them through self-advocacy. Encourage them to reach out to their teachers and ask for help if they need it. Make sure they're fully aware of the accommodations they're entitled to and that they're utilizing them.

Make it a priority to keep up with appointments at the pediatrician and any other medical specialists that care for your child. Communicate new diagnoses and treatment protocols with the school so they can track changes in performance. Consider accessing resources in the community and through your health insurance to obtain services that can help your child flourish. For example, private speech therapy, OT sessions at a sensory gym, and social skills classes can supplement what is being provided at school. In-home ABA therapy can help parents manage behavior more effectively. Hiring a reading tutor or executive function coach can teach your child valuable skills that will carry over into the classroom. For some families, consulting with a nutritionist or chiropractor is the puzzle piece that has the biggest impact. Networking with other parents of children with disabilities in your area can help you access a treasure trove of information about what's available locally.

Now that I've painted a picture of all of the "extras" that parents "should" be doing—and you're probably hyperventilating—here's where I'm going to grant you permission to toss it all out the window if it's not realistic for your family. Try to be really intentional about not overscheduling. Equally important is making sure that everyone has ample opportunity to power down. It's likely that your child will have to work harder at school than his or her peers. And that frustration in some way, shape, or form will be part of their school experience. Therefore, it's important that they get to decompress and recharge their battery on a regular basis. In fact, I can't think of anything else more vital to a child's overall well-being. There are only so many hours in the day. Sleep, play, and family dinners should also be prioritized, in my opinion. You will have to do your best to find the right balance for your family.

Another important job for parents beyond the IEP meeting is to actively identify and nurture the gifts that your child has been given. Let them fully explore the magnificent world outside of school and discover what makes their heart most happy. It might be sports, singing, working with animals, helping young children, fashion design, computer coding, or anything else that lights them up. These talents will be the buoys they cling to when their self-esteem takes a hit. These passions will help them to find their tribes, their communities where they feel accepted and confident. Where they feel special, in a different way.

PART 5

Savvy Advocacy in Action

• • ● ● ● ● • •

Anyone who knows me will tell you that I'm a rainbows and unicorns, glass-half-full kind of gal. I believe that ideals such as peace, unity, empathy, and kindness are what make the world go round. I loathe conflict. If there is ever a rift within my group of girlfriends, I'm the one that jumps in and tries to smooth everything over as quickly as possible. If I had a magic wand, I would literally bring it with me to IEP meetings and wave it around the table until everyone is in complete agreement and smiling. Ahhh, a girl can dream . . .

So you may be thinking to yourself, *well she sure chose an interesting field to go into then!* You see, conflict is at the heart of the work that I do. Typically, a parent isn't contacting me because things are all fine and dandy with their child's IEP. By the time I enter the conversation, things have already started to go downhill. At a minimum, parties aren't seeing eye to eye on a specific issue. At the other extreme, communication has broken down completely, trust has been lost, and you can cut the tension in the meeting room with a knife.

So, my special education mamas, I have bad news, good news, and then some really good news for you. Let's get the bad news over with first. Most parents WILL encounter conflict with their school district at some point along their child's special education journey. It's pretty much inevitable. I mean, think about it. There are hundreds of decisions about programming, services, and accommodations made between the ages of 3 and 21. There are changing needs, a revolving door of educators, and a brand-new list of goals drafted every school year. It's naive to think that there is never going to be a time when parties disagree. So instead of being thrown for a loop when it happens, let's equip you with the strategies necessary to move forward with confidence.

The good news is that there is an advocacy toolbox full of strategies to help parents navigate through the more difficult times. The times when you hear the word no. The times when your motherly intuition is telling you that your child needs X, but the school team firmly insists that he or she needs Y. The times when you feel like you're not being heard and that your concerns aren't being taken seriously. The times when your vision for your child doesn't match the rest of the team's. And definitely for the times when you fear that your child is being harmed in some way.

The REALLY good news is that the same tools and techniques can be used no matter what the specifics of your situation are. I thought it would be helpful to frame each within the context of a real-life conflict that you might encounter. Chapters 18–21 contain some of the most common dilemmas my clients find themselves in. These are challenges I've faced personally as a mother, professionally as an advocate, and that I have helped parents work through when I had their children sitting in my classroom. Let's take a closer look . . .

CHAPTER 17
Your Advocacy Toolbox

. . . .

N-o.

These are the two letters that are the most difficult for a parent to hear when strung together in conversation at the IEP table. You have just explained to the IEP Team why you believe that your child needs X in order to be successful. But instead of looking around the table seeing heads nodding in agreement, you see people shifting uncomfortably in their chairs, with downward gazes. Here it comes.

No comes packaged several different ways, including, "We can't do that," "We don't do that here," and, "We don't think that is warranted at this time." "I'm sorry, but we only have Y available," and, "I will have to ask my supervisor and get back to you," are often no in disguise too. In chapter 15, I provided three of my favorite responses to statements like these, but I want to unpack them even further for you here.

Whether it's no to an evaluation, classification, placement, or service, there is nothing that leaves a parent feeling more defeated and powerless. The image of a squirrel flattened by a Mack truck going full speed comes to mind. You're left thinking, *Is that it? How come they get the final say? Doesn't my opinion matter? Now what?*

To be perfectly honest, sometimes no is the appropriate answer to your request. Sometimes what a parent wants for their child is unnecessary or unreasonable. It's more of a want than a need. Remember the Rolls Royce versus Honda Accord analogy? If you ask for Italian leather interiors and diamond-studded hubcaps, you're going to get shot down. The school is only obligated to provide your child with an education that is appropriate to meet their needs.

A collaborative school team will respect the parents' position though. They will recognize that a no can be an incredibly difficult pill to swallow, and try to soften the blow by offering alternatives whenever possible. In other words, approximations to the request made, without granting the full thing. For example, I once worked with a parent who was seeking the support of a special education teacher in the general education setting for her elementary student with a behavior disability. The school district felt that a shared classroom aide was sufficient. After many meetings and a mediation conference, the district ended up offering a special education teacher for three days a week and the support of a paraprofessional for the other two. Both sides agreed to this compromise and everyone was content.

All that being said, there is a time and place to put on your advocacy hat and ramp up your efforts to pursue exactly what you think your child needs. So how does a parent go about doing that? There are a handful of strategies that you can rely upon time and time again.

Put it in Writing

You're always, always, always going to start by putting your concerns and requests in writing. In an email to your case manager, you will also want to include the specific examples/reasons/data points that you have gathered, in bullet point format. Be as specific as possible. The more objective data you have, the better. Basically, you are putting your concerns in writing to ensure that communication is crystal clear. You're also trying to persuade the team to agree with your point of view. Lastly, you're creating a paper trail in case you decide to contact an attorney and/or file a formal complaint in the future.

Here is the outline of an email I wrote with parents advocating on behalf of their 10-year-old son with severe dyslexia. The bullets are the many sources of data and other evidence that can be used to strengthen one's position. In Johnny's case, we had a statement from the publisher of his literacy program, a line graph comparing his rate of progress to his same-grade peers, the recommendations within our state's Dyslexia Handbook, reports that showed a lack of progress toward his IEP goals, and an independent evaluation to help us make our case. We listed and explained each thoroughly in the body of our email. A carefully constructed letter like this is an extremely powerful advocacy tool. It works! At their next meeting, Johnny's mom was successful in advocating for an increase in reading intervention for her son.

Dear Ms. (case manager),

We are very concerned that Johnny's current IEP is not meeting all of his needs, and that he's falling farther and farther behind his peers in reading. For next year, we're requesting a highly structured, multi-sensory Orton-Gillingham–based reading intervention program, delivered in 1:1 sessions by a certified instructor, 5 days a week for 45 minutes per session.

Below, please find the evidence to support this request:

- *Standardized test scores, benchmark assessment results*
- *Standard scores or percentile ranks from formal evaluation reports*
- *Report card grades and IEP progress reports*
- *Teacher comments on tests, assignments, and via email*
- *Parent observations*
- *Recommendations by experts*
- *Research related to your child's disability*
- *Feedback from tutors*
- *Student input (video, audio, or written)*
- *Notes from classroom observations*

- *Language taken from district policy, state regulations, or federal law*
- *Guidance issued by OSEP via policy letters and memos*

We are requesting an IEP meeting to discuss this further, and look forward to working collaboratively with the rest of the team to create an appropriate plan for Johnny.

Sincerely,

Mr. and Mrs. Smith

Once you've sent your email, a meeting will be scheduled and you will work together to develop a plan. Expect that there will be some back and forth negotiation involved. You can decide ahead of time if you're willing to compromise on any of the issues you've raised or if you plan to take a firm stance.

If things don't go as well as you'd like at the IEP table, there are a few additional strategies to try. You can elevate your concerns up the chain of command by getting an administrator involved. You can ask for written notice, which is one of your parental rights. You can request that a third party facilitator be brought into the conversation. And after all other remedies have been exhausted, you can file a formal complaint. Let's examine each option more closely.

Chain of Command

If you're not seeing eye to eye with the rest of the IEP Team, you can follow the chain of command to appeal to someone in a higher position of authority. From the bottom up, the hierarchy of special education starts with your child's teachers and therapists, then progresses up to the case manager, the director of special services (or a similar title), and finally the superintendent. In larger districts, there may even be a supervisor or two thrown in there. There are also times when it makes sense to reach out to the building principal, especially on matters such as discipline, scheduling, staffing, or safety.

Parents can invite an administrator into the conversation by cc-ing him or her on emails, calling their office directly, or inviting them to attend the next IEP meeting. A word of caution though . . . going "above someone's head" is the equivalent of telling a retail associate that you want to speak to the manager. To make sure you don't create too many waves, you can send a simple explanatory message like this to the IEP Team: *"Good morning. I wanted to let you know that I reached out to the Assistant Superintendent of Special Education after our last meeting. I would like the IEP Team to have the benefit of her expertise and decision-making power as we continue to work together on Cami's IEP."*

In reality, sometimes lower-level educators have their hands tied when it comes to making big decisions. They might even fully agree with what a parent is requesting, but not be able to grant it based on directives issued by their department heads. This is a major obstacle for IEP Teams to overcome, so I wanted to make you aware of it. According to IDEA, there should already be someone in attendance at meetings who is "knowledgeable about the availability of resources . . ." (34 CFR § 300.321(a)(4)). But if I had a dollar for every time I heard the line: "I'm going to have to check with my supervisor and get back to you," I'd be enjoying a shopping spree at HomeGoods right about now.

Prior Written Notice

PWN is your new BFF. Or it should be.

Flip back to chapter 13 to refresh your memory about what it is and when it's used. Written notice is an effective tool because it holds the school district accountable for their actions. If they are refusing to take action on a parental request, there has to be a basis for it, supported by evidence. Written notice requires the school district to slow down, document the rationale behind their decision-making, and acknowledge all options that were considered.

Along with information about how parents can utilize their procedural safeguards, PWN must include these components:

- Description of the action the school district proposes or refuses to take
- Explanation of why the school district is proposing or refusing to take that action
- Description of each evaluation procedure, assessment, record, or report the school district used in deciding to propose or refuse the action

- Description of any <u>other choices</u> that the IEP Team considered and the reasons <u>why</u> those choices were rejected
- Description of <u>other reasons</u> why the school district proposed or refused the action

Speaking from personal experience, big decisions are made at IEP meetings ALL THE TIME and written notice is never provided. Or, districts will include it within the IEP but it falls short of the criteria listed above. Here's where your savvy advocacy skills to come into play. Whenever you hear a no, ask for written notice. Not only will it send a powerful message about accountability, it will become an important part of the paper trail if you ever decide to file a complaint.

Facilitated IEP Meetings

Many states now offer something called a Facilitated IEP Meeting, in which a neutral third party attends in order to encourage positive communication. Ultimately, a facilitator's goal is to help the team create an IEP that everyone is satisfied with. They promote things like active listening, mutual respect, and collaboration. A good facilitator will help an IEP Team avoid two of the biggest pitfalls to productivity: rehashing events from the past, and going in circles around and around on the same issue without moving forward. They will also make sure that there are no personal attacks, shaming, blaming, or finger-pointing when emotions are running high.

The facilitator is not there to take sides or "rule" one way or another. But, they can help ensure that all parties have a chance to be heard. They may even offer suggestions in an attempt to find common ground. IEP facilitation is a free service and can help families avoid more formal dispute resolution processes. In New Jersey, it's offered through our state Department of Education. In other states, it's offered at the county level or within each school district. You'll have to do some digging around to see if FIEP meetings are an option for your family.

Formal Dispute Resolution

After several unsuccessful IEP meetings, if you feel like negotiations have reached a standstill, you can utilize the collection of formal dispute resolution processes spelled out in the IDEA. They are designed to protect the rights of children with disabilities and their parents and come into play when a parent feels that their child's right to a free and appropriate public education has been violated.

If you think this is where your situation is headed, I encourage you to consult with an experienced advocate or an attorney, since your school district will be enlisting the help of their legal team. Otherwise, an untrained parent will be at a significant disadvantage. Many states have a county-wide supervisor of special education that parents can contact with questions. The Office of Special Education within your state's Department of Education can also offer some basic guidance.

Complaint Resolution

Generally speaking, this is a fast and effective route to take if you have strong evidence that a procedural violation occurred. For example, school districts are legally required to provide an interpreter at IEP meetings upon request. Failure to do so is a violation of the parental right to fully participate in the IEP process. If you have evidence that an interpreter was requested within a reasonable amount of time, but one was not provided, the parent could file a complaint against the school district. Following an investigation, the State might rule that another IEP meeting, with an interpreter present, should be held immediately. Unless there are extenuating circumstances, complaints should be resolved within 60 days.

Some other common grounds for a state complaint:

- Failure to have all IEP Team members present at a meeting
- Failure to evaluate in all areas of suspected disability
- Failure to adhere to specified timelines

- Failure to provide written notice
- Failure to follow state guidelines for class size or classroom aides
- Failure to provide a service or modification specified in the IEP

OCR Complaint

It is not only unethical, but also illegal, to discriminate against individuals with disabilities. Doing so is a violation of their most fundamental civil rights. For example, if a child with cerebral palsy was excluded from class field trips because her wheelchair couldn't fit on the school bus, that's not okay. The district is responsible for making sure that students with disabilities receive the same educational benefits as their nondisabled peers. In order to meet this obligation, specialized transportation could have and should have been provided.

All public school students have the right to an equitable education. If you believe that your child was discriminated against at school on the basis of his or her disability, you can file a complaint with the Office of Civil Rights (OCR) within the US Department of Education. Additional information and a Discrimination Complaint Form can be found on their website.

Voluntary Mediation

If you and your school district cannot agree on some aspect of your child's education, either side can file a request for mediation. An independent, unbiased mediator from the state comes to meet with both parties and tries to guide them toward an agreement that is mutually satisfactory. During a mediation conference, the mediator will take the parents and school officials into separate rooms and listen carefully to their different points of view. He or she then brings everyone back together in an effort to bridge the gap. Unlike a FIEP meeting, a mediator has the power to draw up a legally binding agreement on the spot.

Due Process Hearings

If mediation is unsuccessful, the next step is a formal due process hearing. Either a hearing officer or an administrative law judge will preside over the proceedings, which closely resembles a legal trial. Parents may represent themselves in a due process hearing, but I strongly recommend against it. You have now entered the advocacy big leagues. Enlisting the services of an experienced education attorney will give you the best chance of prevailing.

Is there a time and a place for due process? Absolutely. Sometimes it's the only way to secure the education your child is entitled to. But please go into it fully informed, making sure that you've carefully weighed the potential benefits against the drawbacks—namely the expenses that you will incur by retaining an attorney, as well as the cost of your time and emotional energy. Keep in mind that the appeals process is grueling and could take years. What will the ramifications be on your child during that time? Or your finances? Your energy, mental health, and emotional well-being? These are just a few of the many factors to think about.

The system recognizes all of these drawbacks and strongly encourages the development of a settlement agreement prior to going to hearing. As a result, there are several opportunities to resolve differences built-in. For example, within 15 days of an initial parent request for a due process hearing, the district must arrange what's called a **resolution session**. The resolution period remains open for 30 days before progressing toward the actual hearing.

* * *

The sobering reality is that advocating for your child's educational needs is rarely a walk in the park. It's hard work. Sometimes in spite of our best advocacy efforts, a school district is unwilling to budge. Sometimes the truth as we see it doesn't prevail. And wow, is it distressing when these things happen. But as individuals, we get to decide if we're going to get stuck in the injustice of it all or channel our energy in a more positive direction. Sadly, I see too many parents held captive by the former.

There is no such thing as "losing" at the IEP table or in the courtroom. And there is no such thing as "failing" your child either. Sometimes, decisions won't go your way, but I'm fairly certain that doesn't mean that your child is doomed. It might mean that it's time to pivot with your approach though. Maybe it means relocating to a different town. Or that it's time to start a side hustle so you can afford to send him or her to the private school that you think is best. Perhaps it means staying put and making the best of your current situation. Whatever happens, I hope you derive some peace from knowing that you're doing the best you can. And boy oh boy, is your child lucky to have you in their corner!

Throughout your special education journey, there will be plenty of opportunities to turn lemons into lemonade. Take advantage of each and every one. Keep showing up. Keep putting one foot in front of the other. Roll with the punches. Because you know as well as I do that when it comes to our kiddos, giving up is not an option.

CHAPTER 18
What to Do When the IEP Isn't Being Followed

If you've been keeping up with your homework, then you have read over your child's IEP and are fully aware of its contents. So what happens when you suspect or even have concrete proof that it's not being followed? Maybe your child isn't getting the amount of therapy outlined, or isn't receiving an important accommodation. Or perhaps your child needs the support of a 1:1 aide for the entire day, but there isn't another staff member filling in when he or she is absent.

The reality is that educators are human. Sometimes a detail within the IEP is innocently missed, especially at the beginning of the year when they are still getting to know your child. Legally, everyone who works with your child is responsible for making sure the IEP is implemented. This includes general education, special education, and special area teachers as well. As your child gets older, and if they are capable, it will increasingly become their responsibility to self-advocate. But until that point, they need you in their corner.

My first advice is to communicate your concerns as soon as possible. I know it's hard to believe, but sometimes your 7-year-old isn't the most reliable source of information! You're going to need to dig deeper to get the full story, including the school's perspective. Most of the time, a simple email or phone conversation is all it takes. The school will be genuinely grateful that you brought an over-sight to their attention and promise to address it immediately. Problem solved.

For example, suppose your sixth-grader's IEP states that she needs a hard copy of the teacher's notes so she can focus on processing new information instead of note-taking. Trying to do both simultaneously causes major frontal lobe overload for Charley who has ADD. Six weeks into the school year, she drops the bomb that she has a D average in Science class. You stifle the urge to reprimand her for not telling you sooner, and start to investigate. It doesn't take long at all to pinpoint the main issues. First of all, your darling daughter hasn't been using her agenda book, and so there are several assignments that were never completed. Secondly, Charley's binder is a hot mess and there aren't any notes to be found. Again, you resist the temptation to lose your cool.

Instead of turning into the IEP police and firing off a scathing email to the science teacher, you reach out calmly to state that you don't think your child is receiving all of her accommodations. You coach Charley to request the notes from the first unit and the opportunity to retake the test. The teacher apologizes profusely and even offers tutoring sessions after school if needed. You agree to start checking Charley's assignment book and help her organize her binder each night. It's a team effort, but well worth it when she maintains a B+ in Science for the rest of the year.

You should always cc your child's case manager on teacher emails that involve concerns about IEP implementation. If you are unable to resolve the issue by talking to the educator directly, requesting a full IEP Team meeting is the next step. If what your child is telling you still conflicts with what you hear at the meeting, I would continue to pursue the issue. You can gather additional information by requesting a classroom observation, asking for your child's class-work to be sent home, requesting more frequent home-school communication, and by reviewing classroom data collection charts very carefully. Your specific strategy will depend on the situation. A recurrent IEP violation that you can prove is grounds for filing a complaint.

Related Services

The provision of related services is one aspect of special education in which IEPs may not be followed as strictly as they should be. There are a few important factors to keep in mind though. At the beginning of the school year, related services and therapies might not start right away. Educators recognize the value of allowing children the time to bond with their new teachers and classmates, and to get used to classroom rules and routines before they start pulling kids out for sessions. By the end of the second week of school, it's reasonable to expect services to begin.

Make sure you hold the school accountable for providing the correct amount of intervention over the course of the school year. The exact number and length of sessions will be written explicitly in your child's IEP. Some school districts list the sessions per week or month, while others list the total number of sessions for the school year. There are pros and cons to each of these formats. The former lends itself to consistent scheduling, while the latter allows for flexibility around unexpected events, such as student absence, teacher absence, assemblies, field trips, etc. Either way, pay attention to make sure that your child receives the full amount of intervention prescribed in the IEP.

One way to do this is with a simple communication notebook. Whenever your child receives a related service, ask the provider to jot down the date and the skills that were worked on. If they have time, they can even write down some ideas for reinforcement activities at home. You will want to discuss the particulars with the IEP Team in order to make sure that what you're requesting is reasonable. For example, would you rather have your child's speech therapist spend the last five minutes of the session writing a note to you or working with your child on his or her goals? Maybe bi-weekly or monthly communication makes more sense. Or perhaps a template could be created to simplify the process.

One family I work with receives a shared Google Doc with notes from each related service provider and interventionist each week, because that's what was deemed easiest for everyone involved. My own child's speech therapist sends home a half-sheet that probably takes her about 30 seconds to complete, but effectively communicates exactly what I need to know. I can't think of a good reason why a competent therapist would refuse to provide something similar if requested by a parent.

Another common question that I hear relates to whether or not schools are required to schedule make-ups when a session is missed. The oh-so-satisfying answer . . . well, it depends. There is no specific mention in IDEA, but check to see if your district has a written policy on this topic. I had this issue come up recently with one of my families and located the applicable policy on the Board of Education website. It clearly stated that missed sessions due to teacher absence, field trips, and assemblies had to be made up at a later date. Missed sessions due to snow days/delayed openings/early dismissals and student absence did not.

Many advocates, lawyers, and parents lean toward a strict interpretation of the IEP, insisting that a student receive every single minute of every single session the IEP specifies. I appreciate this perspective and have made the exact argument many times. What's written in the IEP should be provided. Period. End of story. But I also see the value in flexibility and the need to consider the big picture when something out of the ordinary occurs. If a child misses half of an OT session one day so she can participate in the pizza party that her class earned for good behavior, I'm down with it! Or if a child misses two speech sessions because she was in Disney World with her family, I don't think the school should be responsible for making it up. You will also need to consider that your child will be missing instruction in another class in order to receive a makeup session. Could that potentially impact him or her more negatively than a missed counseling session? Maybe yes, maybe no. It's going to be situation-specific, so I urge you to consider every angle. Make sure you're clear with the IEP Team about your expectations so everyone is on the same page.

The IEP is a legal document. Failure to adhere to what's written is a clear violation. If you notice a pattern of violations or feel like the school has been less than responsive to your concerns, filing a complaint with your state Office of Special Education is a viable option. They will investigate the allegations you raise and make recommendations accordingly. If they rule that your child was in fact denied services or instruction they were entitled to, **compensatory education** may be offered as a remedy. This can take the form of money to be used to pay for replacement services, or additional hours of instruction scheduled when school is not in session. The intent is to bring the student's performance up to the level it would have been had the absence of instruction never occurred.

As I'm typing this chapter, special education students across the United States are feeling the effects of lost instructional time due to the COVID-19 pandemic. Sadly, behavioral, academic, and social regression is widespread. Students with the highest levels of need, who simply cannot make meaningful progress toward their IEP goals via virtual instruction, have been impacted the most severely. In the cases where a school district has failed to provide an appropriate education, the student should be entitled to compensatory education. At this point, it's hard to predict the extent to which courts will hold school districts accountable. While I expect some leniency to be extended, it is my sincere hope that decision-making is as student-centered as possible.

CHAPTER 19
What to Do When Your Child Isn't Making Progress

The purpose of an IEP is to create the plan by which a child will make progress toward their set of individualized goals. If a child fails to make progress, that's a big problem. It's quite possible that the IEP needs to be revised. In the IDEA's Code of Federal Regulations it states, ". . . the IEP Team revises the IEP, as appropriate, to address any lack of expected progress toward the annual goals . . . and in the general education curriculum, if appropriate" (34 CFR §300.324(b)(1)(ii)(A)). Schools are responsible for convening an IEP meeting, and making revisions in a timely manner, when there are signs that the current plan isn't working.

This is precisely why progress reporting at regular intervals throughout the year is so important. It's one of the best (and only) ways for parents to make sure the IEP is doing what it's supposed to do, and that our children are making educational progress. Unfortunately though, it's not uncommon for me to come across IEP goals that aren't measurable. If a goal isn't measurable, then data can't be collected easily. If numerical data cannot be collected, then it's almost impossible to determine if progress is being made. See how important it is to craft solidly SMART goals for your child's IEP?

I've discovered that way too often, teachers aren't collecting data the way they should be. Furthermore, there isn't anyone holding them accountable for doing so. I was once in an IEP meeting with a veteran special education teacher. I could tell that she was skilled and passionate and I liked her immediately. What I couldn't figure out though was why she appeared to be so nervous the entire time. With over 25 years of experience under her belt, I imagined she had attended hundreds of IEP meetings at that point. Where in the world was all of the anxiety coming from?

After a successful meeting, she pulled me aside as we were walking out and apologized. She shared that never before in her career had she been asked for evidence to show that a student was making progress toward her goals! She hardly slept the night before. My jaw dropped. I stared at her in disbelief. Was this for real?

You see, prior to the meeting, I emailed the case manager to request that the teachers bring their progress monitoring data with them. Jenna's parents were really concerned about their fifth-grade daughter's difficulty with math. The progress reports from her resource room teacher listed either a "PG" for Progressing Gradually or a "PS" for Progressing Satisfactorily, next to each goal. But those descriptors seemed so vague and subjective. The parents wanted to see evidence that her math skills were actually improving. In my opinion, that's an extremely fair, reasonable, and basic request. But apparently, it was one that this teacher had never received, so she panicked. In 25 years, not one parent had ever held her accountable in this way before. Moms, let that sink in . . . it sounds like we have some work to do.

Progress Monitoring

Goals that are well-written lend themselves to data collection that is quantitative. Depending on the skill that you're targeting, you should be able to see an increase or decrease in performance over time to prove that an intervention is working. For example, are test scores increasing? Is the frequency of a targeted inappropriate behavior decreasing? Are reading level and fluency increasing? Is the number of prompts a child needs to complete a task decreasing? Is the number of math facts that a child recalls in one minute increasing? The answers to all of these questions rely on an analysis of the numbers. Progress in all skill areas must be able to be measured in some way.

Various tools, such as running records, curriculum-based assessments, teacher-made quizzes, rubrics, and simple data collection charts, can be used. You can absolutely ask to see what your child's teachers are using. Most importantly, a baseline is established for each goal at the beginning of the year and then measurement is ongoing. Progress must be reported to parents as frequently as is specified in the IEP. Typically, it happens 3–4 times a year, in conjunction with report cards.

Not only does the federal statute governing special education require that students with disabilities make progress, there is case law to support it. In 2017, the Supreme Court of the US (*Endrew F. v. Douglas County School District*) ruled that school districts must ensure *more than minimal progress.* It doesn't quantify it, as every child is unique and should be looked at through an individual lens, but it does mandate a much higher standard for progress than ever seen before. The specific language reads, ". . . progress appropriate in light of the child's circumstances." In other words, if your child is capable of making progress, then your school district is legally responsible for making it happen.

What Now

So, what exactly should you do if you think your child is making less progress than they should, in light of his or her circumstances?

Step 1: Request an IEP Team meeting. Ask the teachers to bring evidence of the progress your child is making. Here's some simple language for your email: "*I would like to schedule an IEP meeting to talk about Madison's performance. I am requesting that each teacher and therapist bring evidence of the progress she's making toward her IEP goals. Thank you!*"

Step 2: Gather any data you have to suggest that your child isn't progressing as much as they should be. This could be an observation journal with notes about your child's performance at home on homework assignments, graded tests and quizzes, or reports from private tutors, therapists, or other experts.

Step 3: At the meeting, carefully review the data that the school provides. Share your concerns and the data you've collected. Try to use the evidence to advocate, as opposed to your emotions.

Step 4: Request an increase in the *intensity* or *frequency* of the current intervention, or suggest a new approach altogether.

Step 5: Work with the IEP Team to create a new plan. Schedule a time to meet again in 6–8 weeks (or earlier if needed) to discuss how it's going.

Final Thoughts

- If there is disagreement about whether or not your child is making reasonable progress, you may need input from a formal evaluation using standardized, objective assessments. You could even request that your child's triennial evaluation date be moved up.

- Sometimes the school will try to use report card grades as evidence of progress made. If this makes you feel uneasy, your intuition is correct. Grades are extremely subjective. They're often calculated to include things like participation, homework completion, and effort, as opposed to representing a pure measure of academic competency. Benchmark assessment results and good progress monitoring data are much more valid measures.

- In most cases of a specific learning disability, your child should not merely be "making progress." In order for it to be *meaningful* progress, you should see the achievement gap starting to close between the student and his or her peers. If they're still performing several grade levels behind as time goes on, you could argue that an increase in the current intervention or a different intervention is needed.

CHAPTER 20
What to Do When You Disagree With Placement

The decision about appropriate placement is arguably the most important that an IEP Team makes. It should come as no surprise that disagreement about it is the number one reason that parents end up in due process. Placement hinges upon the determination of the least restrictive environment (LRE) for the student to be educated in. This is not a simple task. If you recall from chapter 7, the concept of LRE holds that students must be educated alongside their peers in the general education setting to the maximum extent appropriate (CRF 34 §300.114(a)(2)). The word *appropriate* is open to interpretation though, so this is where most of the complexity lies.

When considering placement, the general education classroom is ALWAYS where the discussion begins. Can the student be educated with his or her peers if the necessary accommodations, modifications, and supplementary supports are put in place? If the answer is yes, then boom—you've determined the appropriate placement for the child. Some parents, advocates, and attorneys believe that there is one and only one "least restrictive environment," the general education classroom. Others describe the most appropriate setting for each child, whatever that's determined to be, as the "least restrictive environment." Either way, the goal is the same: to educate children alongside or as close as physically possible to their nondisabled peers.

In my opinion, there are several reasons why removal from the general education setting may be justified. If the child's behavior interferes with their own learning or the learning of other students, even with positive behavior supports in place, a different environment should be considered. Or, if the level of distraction or pace of instruction causes a child overwhelm to the point of harm in the form of overstimulation, extreme anxiety, or frustration, it's not appropriate. Finally, if there is absolutely no way to provide meaningful educational benefit of any kind, the argument for a more restrictive setting can be made. Discussions around the IEP table are often boiled down to a cost-benefit analysis. If more harm than good would be done in the general education classroom, it's time to explore other options. Each child and each set of circumstances are unique though.

If the IEP Team agrees that there is no way to make the general education setting appropriate for your child, the next step is to consider instruction in a smaller classroom with a special education teacher for a portion of the day. Can the student access his or her education in that environment with the necessary modifications, accommodations, and support? If yes, then you've found the appropriate setting. If the answer is still no, you continue in this manner along the continuum of placement options until you get to a yes. The team can also consider a self-contained classroom for the majority of the day, placement in a special program in a local public school district, a private school catering to children with disabilities, and home instruction.

Beware Placements of Convenience

Placement should NEVER be based strictly upon a student's disability or educational classification. It's very possible that two children with the same disability will thrive in very different learning environments. Look no further than the growing population of children on the autism spectrum. The least restrictive setting for one could be inappropriate and even harmful for another. Individual needs determine goals, and a child's goals are what drives specialized instruction and placement. So if it's recommended that your child is placed in the "autism class" or the "behavior disabilities class," your advocate radar should start beeping loudly. Please take the time to learn more about the program, ask all of your questions, and schedule a tour to make sure it really is the proper fit.

Decisions about placement should also NEVER be made based on logistics, such as staffing, space, or the availability of resources. Yes, those are all important factors that school administrators have to juggle behind the scenes, but they do not have a place at the IEP table. I've attended way too many meetings where placement is being discussed and a viable option is crossed off the list because the class is already "full." Or you might hear something along the lines of, "We can't put your child in general education for Math because there isn't a staff member available to support him that period." I've even had to interject at meetings when teachers and administrators go off on a tangent about scheduling and/or staffing. I typically say something like, "I'm sorry to interrupt, but frankly, that's not Spencer's problem. Let's use our time together to discuss Spencer's unique needs and how we're going to meet them in the least restrictive environment." As always, you're going to want to make a statement like this politely; but at the same time, you want to be firm enough to stop the conversation from going down the logistics rabbit hole that is their headache and NOT yours. If the environment that your child needs to receive FAPE does not currently exist, the district is responsible for creating it in-house or finding it out-of-district. Period.

I was once helping a mom advocate on behalf of her ninth-grade son who has dyslexia and extreme anxiety. He had been very successful in the general education setting with the support of a special education co-teacher for the previous five years. At his annual review meeting, we were discussing courses for tenth grade. I looked at the draft IEP and noticed that Josh was recommended for this same placement for all of his content classes again, with the exception of World History. When I questioned the change, his case manager casually explained, "Well, we don't have an in-class support option for tenth-grade History." But the unspoken truth that I also heard was, *"We don't have an extra special education teacher who is available to teach that period."* Say what??? How in the world were they going to justify removing services from a student who struggles with reading and writing in a class that relies so heavily upon both? Did they have evidence to justify the need for less support? Nope. Nada. Zip. Zilch.

Luckily, the story has a happy ending. It took assertive parent advocacy in the form of a request for prior written notice, a follow-up email documenting what was discussed and parental concerns, and a phone call with the supervisor of Special Services to make things right. The school ended up hiring an additional part-time special education teacher, and Josh (and his classmates with IEPs) received the appropriate instruction for World History.

What alarms me the most is that I catch "little" things like this happening all the time. If a parent isn't paying close enough attention, fully aware of their rights and able to advocate effectively, their child could miss out on something they need and deserve. That being said, there is no need to panic, nor live in fear that your school district is trying to "get one over on you." If you take a proactive advocacy stance from Day 1 and show up throughout the IEP process, you will be able to iron out wrinkles like these with confidence.

Advocating for Inclusion

One benefit to remaining in the general education setting is access to neurotypical peer models. As educators, we know that providing children with the opportunity to learn from each other is key. Further, that the development of communication skills and prosocial behavior stems largely from observation and imitation, especially in the early years. So when a student is educated in more restrictive environments, they risk missing out on critical learning experiences.

Another advantage is access to the general education curriculum. When children are placed in self-contained settings, families and teachers can lose sight of grade level expectations without even realizing it. The craft of being a good special education teacher is a tricky balancing act for this reason. You never want to over-modify or over-accommodate to a student's detriment. When I was a resource room teacher, I tried to be intentional about planning out units and lessons with my general education colleagues. I needed the perspective of what my students' same-grade peers were learning and accomplishing so I could hold the bar as high as possible for all of us. As the parent member of the IEP Team, you can help by becoming familiar with your child's grade level standards to ensure that goals are ambitious enough. If you see that your child has met a goal mid-year, you can request that mastery criteria be elevated or that a loftier goal be added in order to extend learning even further.

If you want to advocate for your child to move to a less restrictive setting, you can start by researching the many benefits of inclusion. There is an abundance of it. And then bring this evidence with you to your next IEP meeting. Inclusion is easiest to accomplish in grades PreK–2, when classrooms and activities are more developmental in nature and socialization is actually part of the curriculum. Once a child gets older, the pace of instruction picks up and content demands become more challenging. There will be a much larger gap between what some students are able to achieve compared to their peers. Although meaningful inclusion in the upper grades can be trickier to achieve, it's not impossible.

When my younger son was starting out in our district's preschool program, I wasn't happy with any of the classroom options that were presented. None of them offered the opportunity for inclusion, which I knew was exactly what Luke needed. And so, I googled my heart out and brought a mountain of articles touting the benefits of positive peer models for preschool children to his next IEP meeting. The evidence was objective and compelling. I was also prepared with a list of three excellent schools in our area that had availability and would be thrilled to welcome my family. Thankfully, the story has a happy ending. The very next day, Luke was granted an appropriate private preschool placement that met all of his needs, paid for by the district. What he needed didn't exist, so we worked together as an IEP Team to create it.

No matter what your child's educational placement, you can still advocate for him or her to have as much interaction with peers at school as possible. What is your child's favorite subject? That's a great place to start brainstorming with the team about inclusion opportunities. What are their academic strengths?

If full-time general education isn't a good fit, are there particular lessons or units of study that they could participate in meaningfully? I always encourage parents to come to meetings prepared to offer creative ideas and suggestions. Keep thinking out of the box and watch as the team meets you halfway and starts to do the same.

Several school districts that I work with have incredible programs that match children with higher levels of need with trained peer "buddies." Some organize lunch bunches or unified gym and art classes. Others have after-school clubs where students can make friends, practice social skills, and just have fun with other kids their age. In my experience, these programs are extremely popular; there are even waiting lists for buddy volunteers. The entire school community is impacted in positive, beautiful ways by inclusion.

If nothing like this already exists, I'm here to encourage parents to reach out to the powers that be and volunteer to help create it. Launching new projects and programs takes time and energy, two things that the busy administrators I know don't have an excess of. So if a group of parents really got behind an initiative and even offered to do most of the legwork, I'd be shocked if the idea wasn't well-received. Working in partnership like this is what public school education should be all about. I'm not coming from a place of wishful thinking here. I've lived it firsthand.

In the early years of our SEPAC group, we saw a need to educate the student body about disabilities in the hopes that it would bring about increased inclusion and understanding. After brainstorming with staff members, the idea for Abilities Awareness month was born. We wanted to shift the focus from learning only about differences, to also celebrating ALL children and the abilities that make each one unique. Over the years, the campaign has grown to include hallway murals, lessons about disabilities at every grade level, assemblies, motivational speakers, and hands-on activity days. The staff members at each school have really taken the original idea and run with it. It has been such a wonderful example of home-school partnership in our community, and something everyone is proud of. I'm reminded of the words of Margaret Mead, "Never underestimate the power of a small group of committed people to change the world. In fact, it is the only thing that ever has." Parents, you are not powerless in advocating for and helping to create the school experiences that you desire for your children.

Advocating for a Change in Placement

As a member of the IEP Team, you have the right to participate fully in the conversation about your child's placement. If you feel like decisions are being made unilaterally, or that your opinion doesn't hold as much weight, that's not okay. It's time to give yourself a pep talk if necessary and start getting more assertive. Please don't ever fear judgment or the perception that you're being a "difficult" parent. Let's call it what it is—smart and savvy advocacy.

If you're advocating for your child to receive an out-of-district placement, be prepared to make an ironclad argument. You should think strongly about hiring an experienced advocate or attorney to assist you. In an ideal world it wouldn't even be a factor, but decisions about placement do have a financial component to them. The cost to send a student to a specialized school is very high—upwards of $50,000 per year, in some cases. The harsh reality is that special education is costly, and school districts are underfunded . . . you do the math!

As a result, more and more school districts are creating programs in-district to educate students with more complex needs. For example, ABA-based autism programs, emotional support programs, and highly structured interventions for dyslexia now exist in many public schools. By investing in programs such as these, districts save money and students are educated in their home communities, with increased opportunities for inclusion. In theory, it's a win-win. But sometimes, in spite of their best efforts, what a school district can provide simply isn't enough. Some students require more structure, more intensive intervention, and a more specialized support staff.

To strengthen your case for a change in placement, these are the advocacy strategies to consider.

1) **Gather evidence.**

Basically, you're going to need to gather as much data as humanly possible in order to bolster your position. It's not going to be enough to say, "I think my child will get a better education at Excellent School Academy, so I want him to go there." It doesn't matter what you "want," "think," or "feel," or what the school district "wants," "thinks," or "feels." Rather, it matters much more what the experts say and what the numbers show. The more objective the reasoning, the better.

Specifically, look for evidence that your child isn't making progress in his or her current setting. Look for evidence that all of their needs are not being met. Look for evidence that the district isn't fulfilling their obligation to prepare your child for "further education, employment, and independent living." If the school can prove that there is an appropriate IEP in place, that they are implementing it properly, and that your child is making progress toward his or her goals, you're going to have an uphill battle convincing them (and a judge, if it gets to that) that a change in placement is justified.

2) **Obtain an Independent Educational Evaluation (IEE).**

An evaluation conducted by an independent medical, developmental, or educational expert can be extremely helpful in your advocacy efforts. After the school district conducts an evaluation of your child, if you disagree with the results or believe that they're incomplete, you're entitled to request an IEE at public expense. If they agree, the IEE would be conducted by an expert of your choosing that is not affiliated with the school district, and the school district will pay for it. If the district denies your request for an IEE, they are obligated to file due process against you. At any time, you could also pay out of pocket or use your private insurance to pay for an independent evaluation and then share the reports with the IEP Team.

The IEE is one of my absolute favorite advocacy techniques, but I find that most parents have no idea that the option even exists. A thorough, well-written evaluation report will contain not only the scores from every assessment tool used, but also an interpretation of what the numbers actually mean. It will identify the student's strengths, as well as the areas of greatest need. Notably, an evaluation by an appropriately credentialed professional might yield an official diagnosis, such as autism, dyslexia, oppositional defiant disorder, ADHD, auditory processing disorder, or generalized anxiety. Make sure that you determine the best type of evaluator(s) for your child among the varied options out there. Often, a licensed neuropsychologist is helpful since they have experience with many different learning profiles and have a long list of standardized assessment tools at their fingertips. It really depends on your child and your primary areas of concern though.

Perhaps most valuable, an IEE report will include school-based recommendations for the IEP Team to consider. For example, the evaluator might recommend a specific reading program, a communication device or other types of assistive technology, the frequency and intensity of related services, and the most appropriate educational placement based on their findings. So, now all of a sudden you have so much more than just your own biased opinion about what your child needs. Now there is a professional adding their objective two cents to the mix. If the expert substantiates what you're requesting for your child, your argument just got a whole lot more powerful.

According to IDEA, the IEP Team only has to "consider" the information provided by an independent evaluation, even one that they pay for. They are under no obligation to agree with or follow its recommendations. In my experience though, it's highly unlikely that the report will be dismissed completely. In fact, an advocate, attorney, or knowledgeable parent could effectively argue that doing so would be a violation of parental rights and special education law. An independent evaluation gives a parent much more leverage at the IEP table. You're no longer a solo act. Now you've got some talented backup dancers with strong vocals to enhance your performance.

3) **Tour potential placements.**

Ask to tour a range of placement options so you can get a better sense of what's available. In order to be an informed member of the IEP Team, it's important to know what other programs offer and how they differ. Request to take a look at the programs in-district, within other public school districts in your area, and specialized day schools. If there is a particular placement that you want to see, let your child's case manager know so they can arrange a visit. Make sure you take lots of notes along the way. What did you see that you loved? What turned you off? Which setting would be the best fit for your child, in your opinion? Why? What is your gut telling you? Seeing the different environments firsthand will help clarify the option that you want to advocate for.

4) **Schedule a classroom observation.**

If you're concerned that your child's current environment is not appropriate, look for evidence with your own two eyes. Is he or she frequently off-task? Disruptive? Confused? Hyperactive? Bored? Jot down specific examples. What else do you notice about the learning environment? How many students are in the class? Is the classroom loud and messy or quiet and organized? What effect does that have on your child? How much support did they require? What modifications or accommodations did you see provided?

There's a chance that when you take an up-close look like this, many of your fears will fall by the wayside. You'll observe that your child is actively engaged and appears very happy. You'll see a teacher in action who is responsive to your child's needs and doing an effective job of meeting them. That would be the best-case scenario. On the flip side, you might come away more resolved than ever to advocate for a change. And now you have a list of specific examples to help make your case.

Unfortunately, the presence of a parent in the classroom can have a funny way of affecting the child's behavior. The student either goes into "show-off" mode and becomes a star pupil, or is so distracted that their attention goes out the window. You'll catch these kids looking back at their parents smiling, giggling, and waving about a million times instead of focusing on the lesson.

Or if they're older and more socially aware, don't be surprised if your child feels uncomfortable or even humiliated by your presence. All of these scenarios are less than desirable if you really want to get an accurate snapshot of your child's performance.

Your child's case manager or an administrator might use all of the above as their basis to try to deny your request for an observation. The other excuse that I've heard is their obligation to preserve the privacy rights of the other students in the class. If you encounter this type of resistance, do not back down. Be prepared to suggest alternatives. How about asking to watch the classroom virtually, via an app like FaceTime? Or, if you are working with an advocate, request that they be permitted to conduct the observation in your place. I've done this many times with success. The students have no idea who I am or what I'm doing there and forget all about me after a minute or two. There is zero disruption caused.

5) **Ask for Written Notice.**

Whenever a school district proposes a change in placement or refuses to grant a parent's request for a change in placement, they must provide the parent with formal written notice of their position. You can look back to chapters 13 and 17 for an overview of what should be included. This notice will become important if you decide to move forward with litigation on the issue.

Final Thoughts About Placement

If you disagree with a proposed change in placement, filing a due process petition will freeze the current placement until either you withdraw your petition, a settlement agreement is reached, or a judge issues a ruling. The legal term for this is **Stay Put** or "pendency." Time is of the essence here. Your state will specify the timeline that must be followed, so make sure you research it thoroughly and are crystal clear on your rights. For example, in New Jersey, a parent has 15 days from the time they receive written notice of a change in placement to file for due process before a new IEP goes into effect. Consulting with an attorney at this point is highly advisable.

CHAPTER 21
What to Do When Behavior Isn't Being Managed Effectively

The topic of behavior is one of the most complicated in special education. The reality is that there are many students sitting in classrooms across America with behavior that is challenging to manage. Why is this? For one, there is a growing mental health crisis that has yet to be addressed effectively. There are also children being raised in dangerous or unstable environments who carry a significant trauma history with them as a result. Lastly, there are children who have been diagnosed with a disability that impacts their behavior in negative ways.

I don't believe that there is such a thing as a "bad kid." I do believe that behavior is a form of communication. Maybe a student is acting out simply because they are bored, or maybe they're frustrated because the work is too hard for them. Or maybe they have a short attention span, their body wants to move, they can't regulate their emotions, or they're craving attention. Perhaps they're hungry, they're tired, they're worried, they're sad, or they're easily overstimulated. Instead of merely doling out consequences when behavior problems occur, parents can urge the IEP Team to dig deeper into the root causes. When the cause of an inappropriate behavior is accurately identified, various strategies can be used at home and school to try to shape it. Once positive replacement behaviors are taught and a child learns more acceptable ways to communicate, behavior will improve.

Most schools have a school-wide behavior program that the majority of students buy into. Kids are motivated by positive reinforcement, praise, and public recognition when positive character traits and behaviors are displayed. At the same time, a consequence hierarchy is established for the times when a rule is broken. For example, a warning might be given out initially, followed by a parent phone call, lunch detention, after-school detention, loss of privileges, and suspension. Expectations are often communicated broadly via a Code of Conduct that parents and students sign every school year. For some students though, all of this is not enough. More individualized behavioral management strategies are needed.

Functional Behavior Assessments

Remember how school districts are obligated to evaluate in all areas of suspected disability? If a child's behavior cannot be successfully managed by the classroom teacher with the support of the principal and other staff members, and the behavior is interfering with their own learning or the learning of their classmates, it's time for a formal evaluation called a **Functional Behavior Assessment (FBA)**. If it hasn't already been suggested by your school team, parents can request one in writing. In my experience, the best FBAs are conducted by experts in behavior called **Board Certified Behavior Analysts (BCBAs)**. Larger school districts will likely have an expert in behavior on staff. If not, this service can be contracted out to a private agency.

During an FBA, a student's behavior is closely observed in various environments and a large amount of data is collected. Professionals in the field are trained to recognize both the antecedents of behavior, or what happens immediately before, and the consequences. After a careful analysis of this information, the function, or purpose, of a behavior is identified. Subsequently, the BCBA will design interventions in order to decrease the occurrence of troublesome behavior moving forward.

Behavior Intervention Plan

IEPs have a section designated specifically for behavioral modifications and interventions. If your child has a history of behavioral challenges, make sure it isn't left blank. A **Behavior Intervention Plan (BIP)** is a formal, written plan designed to help modify a student's behavior. If an FBA was conducted, the results and recommendations will be used to create the BIP. A well-written BIP includes strategies to recognize behavioral triggers and prevent further escalation. It should also detail the specific procedures to follow when inappropriate behavior does occur. Commonly, the exact prompts and scripts for the interventions are included.

The BIP should become a part of the student's IEP so it can be implemented throughout the school day to the greatest extent possible. Consistency is key. Ongoing data collection will be important in order to measure its continued effectiveness. The IEP Team, in consultation with the BCBA, parents, and teachers, will then review the data regularly and make adjustments as needed. A good question to ask when a BIP is first created is, *"How frequently will data be collected, analyzed, and reported back to the rest of the team?"* Ongoing communication is your opportunity to monitor what's happening in school while holding the district accountable for meeting your child's behavioral needs. If feedback is not being provided on a regular basis, request it.

Manifestation Determination

Contrary to popular belief, children with IEPs are not exempt from disciplinary action. If a student violates the school's Code of Conduct, then an appropriate consequence is justified. If, however, the behavior can be tied directly to the child's disability, it's a little more complicated.

For example, is your child's ADHD-related impulsivity responsible for his or her disruptive behavior in the classroom and reckless behavior on the playground? Are your child's biting incidents a by-product of his or her need for oral sensory input? Are the fights in the hallway that your teenager keeps getting into stemming from his or her difficulty with emotional regulation? Is chronic tardiness related to your child's social anxiety? I think we can all agree that disruptive behavior, biting, fighting, and lateness are not acceptable. None of these incidents should be excused simply because the child has a special education classification. Ideally, the IEP Team should be working together to determine appropriate consequences for each scenario. A BIP can be created if necessary; or if one already exists, parents can advocate for additional supports and strategies to be added.

When behavioral violations are severe enough to trigger a "change in placement," children with disabilities do have access to additional rights. If a child is suspended for 10 days or more in one school year, that also constitutes a change in placement. In both of these scenarios, a **Manifestation Determination** meeting must be held in order to answer the question: *Is the student's behavior a manifestation of their disability?* If the team gathered (including parents) determines that the answer is yes, then the child is not subject to the same disciplinary action their peers would be. Instead, an FBA must be conducted and a BIP developed without delay. Similarly, if it's determined that the school district failed to manage the behavior effectively, then they must take immediate action to remedy the situation. For extreme situations in which drugs, weapons, and serious bodily harm are involved, there is more of a zero tolerance policy, even for children with disabilities.

I once worked with the family of a second-grader who had already been suspended twice, and it was only the beginning of October. Also troubling, he spent several hours each day sitting in the principal's office. Paul's parents were frequently asked to pick him up from school early due to extreme misbehavior that included spitting at teachers, throwing chairs, and cursing. Clearly, this child's behavior wasn't being managed effectively, and the list of people paying the price was a long one. Most notably, the disabled 7-year-old child whose needs weren't being met and wasn't learning very much. But also, Paul's parents, who were using up sick days and vacation time every time Paul was suspended or was sent home early; the other students in the classroom who were being distracted on a daily basis and at times, in physical danger due to their classmate's aggressive outbursts; and the teachers, guidance counselor, social worker, and principal who spent hours each day with Paul. Without access to appropriate resources and a solid BIP in place, none of them could do their jobs effectively. Once restraint techniques started being used, Paul developed a severe case of anxiety. He no longer felt safe and was afraid to go back to school. To be honest, it was one of the most upsetting situations I have ever seen in a public school; it was traumatic for everyone involved.

I'm thrilled to report that Paul's story turned around dramatically. I think his rock star mom and I used almost every single advocacy strategy in this book, and it didn't happen overnight, but we were successful in creating real change. We held the school district accountable for providing an appropriate education for Paul, and wouldn't you know it, they rose to the challenge and exceeded our expectations. We requested a Manifestation Determination hearing. Additional assessments were completed (including an FBA), highly trained experts in behavior management were brought in for 20 hours each week, and we experimented with different classroom options. I was floored by how quickly and favorably Paul responded to these interventions. I'm not saying that it's smooth sailing 100 percent of the time now, but things are light-years better than they were, and I have hope for even brighter days ahead. Using the tools in your advocacy toolbox, you can help write a success story for your child too.

A CALL TO ACTION

Mothers are the most enthusiastic cheerleaders their children will ever have. It's who we are. How we're wired. We have this endless abundance of perfect love for our babies that pulses through every single cell and muscle fiber. It's quite powerful. Magical almost.

It's what gives us the energy to drag ourselves out of bed at 2:00 a.m. to feed a crying newborn, and to play house just one more time, for the 87th time. It sustains us through the turbulent teenage years when our sweet babies aren't so sweet to us anymore. When they challenge us to keep loving them with the same intensity and devotion. Moms take all of these challenges and meet them. We dig deep and find a way. Every time.

I want you to tap into this same bottomless sea of maternal energy and channel it toward your advocacy efforts. Picking up this book was a great first step. *Now it's time to take action.* Start small. Take the one idea that resonated with you the most for a test drive. Write that email. Request an IEP review meeting. Start a communication log. Join a parent group. Organize your paper trail. Express gratitude. Ask the questions. And then build from there.

Every Picasso painting started with a single brushstroke. And every marathon starts by taking a single first step. And then another. And then another. Millions of tiny steps are strung together until the runner crosses the finish line. They did it. They accomplished something spectacular, one tiny action at a time. And so can you.

Moms, embrace wherever you are right now on your special education journey. You're exactly where you're supposed to be. Embrace your children exactly where they are on their journeys too. Lean into the process of becoming a more savvy advocate. It most definitely is a process, so please be gentle with yourself along the way.

Just. Keep. Going.

Keep growing. Keep moving forward. Celebrate each victory with robust enthusiasm. Even the little ones. *Especially* the little ones. Don't forget to shake your pom-poms.

You've got this.

AFTERWORD

2020.

Aka, the year the rule book flew out the window.

I edited this book during the crazy quarantine summer of 2020. The summer of COVID-19. The summer after special education turned into the Wild, Wild West.

I kept thinking to myself, wow . . . so many of the problems I'm helping to solve here seem trivial all of a sudden. So much of the wisdom that I spent nearly two years crafting into words became grossly insufficient in an instant. In the context of this strange, new world we find ourselves in, uncertainty reigns supreme.

Brand-new challenges have been thrown at the parents of children with disabilities. At the same time, physical safety has replaced student achievement as the number one priority for educators and administrators. And all of us are in the same boat trying to tame a new beast named virtual learning. Basically, the special education landscape changed completely—and overnight.

Questions about FAPE and IEP changes and compensatory education started flooding my inbox. Time and time again I heard myself saying things like, *I just don't know. There is nothing in IDEA about virtual learning. There is no case law that addresses the rights of students during a global pandemic.*

At the time of writing, guidance from the federal and state departments of education has been spotty and nebulous. The Commissioner of Education stated early on that she would not issue any waivers to IDEA, and that IEPs were expected to be implemented to the greatest extent possible. Okay, great . . . but how? I saw some school districts scramble into action while others suffered fear and paralysis and tried to get parents to sign their child's rights away. Some got scrappy, innovative, and really showed up, while others offered little to no instruction for the final three months of the 2019–2020 school year. I saw some students thrive in their new virtual "placements" while others struggled immensely. Across the state and across the country, other advocates reported the same disparities. It was a mess.

The children with the highest levels of need were impacted the most. The fact of the matter is that many, many children just cannot fully access their education through a computer screen, no matter how hard their teachers and parents try. Six-hour school days were replaced by a 15-minute Zoom session because some students simply cannot sit still and attend for longer than that. And packets. So many packets. It didn't take long for fears of academic regression to become a reality. Self-injurious behavior increased for the many children with IEPs who thrive on consistency and structure. Anxiety was pretty much universal, but no one experienced it more acutely than these children whose worlds were just turned completely upside down. Some of what I witnessed was heartbreaking.

You know what this has taught me and continues to teach me as I'm typing this and we're still in the thick of it? Developing your Special Education Savvy has NEVER been more important. The time to get serious about learning this stuff is NOW. The time to lean on the relationship you've built with your school district is NOW. The time to follow your Communication Commandments most religiously is NOW. The time to protect your child's educational rights most fiercely is NOW. The time to make sure your child's vehicle keeps moving forward at an appropriate pace on their education journey is NOW.

The consequences of inaction are far too great.

Pleading ignorance is not an option.

Your child needs you.

You can do this.

With gratitude,

Mary Beth

ACKNOWLEDGEMENTS

This book was a labor of love for two full years. It wouldn't be in your hands right now without the help of many . . .

To Ken, for being an unwavering support system while I spent hours and hours and hours typing away. Thank you for always believing in me and all of my endeavors. I love you!

To Luke and Kenny, for being my inspiration and motivation in all things. Being your mom is my greatest honor. Thank you for not killing each other or eating all of the junk food in the house while Mommy was busy "working on her book." Thanks for cheering me on every step of the way—I did it!

To Stacey, my soul sister from another mister for the past 18 years. From the classroom to motherhood to Congress Hall and every single space in between, your friendship has been a gift. Thank you for your loving enthusiasm throughout this book project.

To my tribe of moms whom I've had the honor of walking with. Thank you for your wisdom, your candor, and for impacting me more than you know. Shout out to the original SEPAC squad: Kathy, Kelly, Kristin, Val, Caroline, Julie, Tara, Kim, Hina, Jeanine, Teah, Beth, and Heather.

To the amazing moms and dads who have invited me along on the special education journey with them and their most precious treasures. Thank you for trusting me and for showing up and doing the work.

To the general education and special education teachers of the world, for their patient, compassionate, and skillful dedication to the students with learning differences in their classrooms. Thank you to the early intervention specialists, OTs, PTs, speech therapists, behaviorists, paraprofessionals, aides, nurses, administrators, counselors, school psychologists, learning consultants, reading specialists, case managers, and bus drivers who advocate for our kiddos every single day. It truly takes a village. I see you all and I thank you.

To my students. Thank you for challenging me, making me smile, and for being my greatest teachers.

To Lydia, Rachael, and Rich, for your servant's hearts. Thank you for giving me the opportunity to live out my passion and purpose.

To the experts who helped me bring this creation into the world: Alexa Bigwarfe from Write Publish Sell, Michelle Fairbanks from Fresh Designs, and the teams from First Editing and BookBaby. Thank you for your guidance during my first author adventure!

APPENDIX

Student Snapshot

Name

1 PERSONAL STRENGTHS	**4** ACADEMIC NEEDS

2 INTERESTS	**5** SOCIAL/EMOTIONAL NEEDS

3 ACADEMIC STRENGTHS	**6** STRATEGIES THAT WORK

MOTHER

FATHER

CONTACT INFO

CONTACT INFO

PARENT RESOURCES

The happiest and most successful parent advocates are open to learning, growing, and connecting. Here are a few of my favorite books, websites, blogs, and podcasts to help you do just that. Many of these authors and resources also have active social media pages. Look for them on your favorite platforms and start engaging with their communities!

Websites with General Information about Disabilities and Special Education

Center for Parent Information & Resources
Your central "hub" of information created for the network of Parent Centers serving families of children with disabilities. (www.parentcenterhub.org)

Child Mind Institute
An independent, national nonprofit dedicated to transforming the lives of children and families struggling with mental health and learning disorders. They offer information and resources for both families and educators. (www.childmind.org)

Parent to Parent USA
These programs offer parent to parent support as a core resource for families with children who have a special health care need, disability, or mental health concern. Through a one-to-one "match," experienced support parents provide

emotional support to families and assist them in finding information and resources. (www.p2pusa.org)

Smart Kids with Learning Disabilities

Helping children with learning and attention differences reach their full potential by inspiring, educating and empowering parents to help their children succeed. They are committed to helping them become effective advocates for their children. (www.smartkidswithld.org)

Understood

This is my #1 favorite website to recommend to the one in five parents of children with learning and attention issues throughout their journey. They offer an abundance of information and tips, and do it in an extremely parent-friendly way. (www.understood.org)

Websites with an Emphasis on Special Education Law

CADRE: Center for Appropriate Dispute Resolution in Special Education

CADRE's major emphasis is on encouraging the use of mediation, facilitation, and other collaborative processes as strategies for resolving disagreements between parents and schools. (www.cadreworks.org)

COPAA: Council of Parent Attorneys and Advocates

COPAA's mission is to protect and enforce the legal and civil rights of students with disabilities and their families. One of their primary goals is to promote excellence in advocacy. A must-have resource for the more advanced parent advocate. (www.copaa.org)

A Day in our Shoes

Lisa Lightner, a devoted mom and non-attorney special education advocate, offers support, information, resources and advocacy assistance to parents who are raising children with disabilities and IEPs. She also runs a very popular Facebook page called *Don't IEP Alone*. (www.adayinourshoes.com)

Wrightslaw

The go-to site for information about special education law, education law, and advocacy for children with disabilities. You can search by topic to find articles, information about cases, and links to resources to learn more. (www.wrightslaw.com)

Disability-Specific Websites

ADDitude: Inside the ADHD Mind

Expert guidance and support for living better with ADHD and related mental health conditions. They also publish a popular magazine which they describe as "required reading for anyone touched by ADHD." (www.additudemag.com)

Apraxia Kids

The largest, most comprehensive and trusted website for information on childhood apraxia of speech (verbal dyspraxia, developmental apraxia of speech) and children's speech and language topics – including evaluation, speech therapy, research and other childhood communication topics. (www.apraxia-kids.org)

The Arc

The Arc's mission is to promote and protect the human rights of people with intellectual and developmental disabilities and actively support their full inclusion and participation in the community throughout their lifetime. They have local chapters in every state across the US. (www.thearc.org)

CHADD: Children and Adults with Attention-Deficit/Hyperactivity Disorder

A clearinghouse for evidence-based information on ADHD, with a focus on support, education and advocacy. (www.chadd.org)

Disability Scoop

The nation's largest news organization devoted to covering developmental disabilities. With daily coverage of autism, intellectual disability, cerebral palsy, Down syndrome and more, no other news source offers a more timely and comprehensive take on the issues that matter to the developmental disability community. (www.disabilityscoop.com)

International Dyslexia Association

Their mission is to create a future for all individuals who struggle with dyslexia and other related reading differences so that they may have richer, more robust lives and access to the tools and resources they need. They also provide information about Decoding Dyslexia groups around the country. (www.dyslexiaida.org)

Learning Ally: Transforming the Lives of Early and Struggling Learners

A leading nonprofit education solutions organization that transforms the lives of early and struggling learners through proven solutions from Pre-K through high school. They also offer a comprehensive audiobook library to support struggling readers. (www.learningally.org)

Learning Disabilities Association of America

LDA visualizes a world in which learning disabilities are universally understood, so all individuals are accepted, supported, and empowered to live a self-determined life. They offer resources for parents, educators, and students. (www.ldaamerica.org)

LD OnLine

A leading website on learning disabilities, learning disorders and differences. They seek to help children and adults reach their full potential by providing accurate and up-to-date information and advice about learning disabilities and ADHD. (www.LDonline.org)

STAR Institute for Sensory Processing Disorder

Their mission is to improve the quality of life for children, adolescents and adults with SPD, and their families. Their website provides comprehensive research and resources for parents. (www.spdstar.org)

TACA: The Autism Community in Action

Provides education, support and hope to families living with autism. Their Mentor Program offers experienced, trained, supported, qualified mentors to guide new parents on the autism journey. (www.tacanow.org)

Books

Differently Wired: A Parent's Guide to Raising an Atypical Child with Confidence and Hope by Debbie Reber

The Dyslexic Advantage: Unlocking the Hidden Potential of the Dyslexic Brain by Brock L. Eide and Fernette F. Eide

Dyslexia Advocate!: How to Advocate for a Child with Dyslexia within the Public Education System by Kelli Sandman-Hurley

The Dyslexia Empowerment Plan: A Blueprint for Renewing Your Child's Confidence and Love of Learning by Ben Foss

The Explosive Child: A New Approach for Understanding and Parenting Easily Frustrated, Chronically Inflexible Children by Ross W. Greene

Helping Your Child with Language-Based Learning Disabilities: Strategies to Succeed in School and Life with Dyslexia, Dysgraphia, Dyscalculia, ADHD, and Processing Disorders by Daniel Franklin

Late, Lost and Unprepared: A Parents' Guide to Helping Children with Executive Function by Joyce Cooper-Kahn and Laurie C. Dietzel

Lost at School: Why Our Kids with Behavioral Challenges are Falling Through the Cracks and How We Can Help Them by Ross W. Greene

The Out-of-Sync Child: Recognizing and Coping with Sensory Processing Disorder by Carol Stock Kranowitz

Overcoming Dyslexia (2020 edition) by Sally Shaywitz

Raising a Sensory Smart Child: The Definitive Handbook for Helping your Child with Sensory Processing Issues by Lindsey Biel and Nancy Peske

Smart but Scattered: The Revolutionary "Executive Skills" Approach to Helping Kids Reach Their Potential by Peg Dawson

Taking Charge of ADHD, Third Edition: The Complete, Authoritative Guide for Parents by Russell A. Barkley

Ten Things Every Child with Autism Wishes You Knew by Ellen Notbohm

The Reason I Jump: The Inner Voice of a 13-Year Old Boy with Autism by Naoki Higashida

Uniquely Human: A Different Way of Seeing Autism by Barry M. Prizant

Wrightslaw: From Emotions to Advocacy: The Special Education Survival Guide by Peter and Pamela Wright

What to Do When You Worry Too Much: A Kid's Guide to Overcoming Anxiety (What-to-Do Guides for Kids) by Dawn Huebner

Parent Blogs

Finding Cooper's Voice

A safe, humorous, caring and honest place where you can celebrate the unique challenges of parenting a special needs child. Prepare to fall in love with Cooper, his mom and their family. (www.findingcoopersvoice.com)

Love That Max

A blog for parents of kids with special needs. Includes posts about parenting children with cerebral palsy and developmental delays. (www.lovethatmax.com)

Noah's Dad

Noah's Dad is giving the world a window into what life is like raising a child born with Down Syndrome. The blog shares facts, information, therapy resources, and lots more. (www.noahsdad.com)

Podcasts

Mama Bear Podcast

A place for women raising children with special needs to get together and chat about life. Mary Susan McConnell and her guests discuss the beautiful highs and the extreme lows that can come with parenting on such unique journeys.

Tilt Parenting: Raising Differently Wired Kids

Parenting activist, speaker, and author Debbie Reber conducts interviews aimed at inspiring, informing, and supporting parents raising differently-wired kids (giftedness, ADHD, Asperger's, 2e, learning differences, sensory processing issues, anxiety, and more).

Parenting ADHD Podcast

Penny Williams, from Parenting ADHDandAutism.com, reveals her powerful parenting strategies, ADHD management tips, and hard-won wisdom so you can get ahead of the curve, to parent your child successfully.

GLOSSARY OF TERMS

Accommodations

The removal of barriers in order to provide your child with equal access to learning. Unlike modifications, accommodations don't change *what* your child is learning. Rather, they change *how* your child is learning.

Assistive technology (AT)

Any device, equipment, or software that helps a student learn, communicate, and function better in school. Examples include everything from low tech items such as walkers, pencil grips, and fidgets, to high tech items such as computer apps and speech-to-text software.

Board Certified Behavior Analyst (BCBA)

A behavior expert with a certification in applied behavior analysis (ABA). They are trained to analyze student behavior across various settings, conduct FBAs and develop BIPs.

Behavior intervention plan (BIP)

An individualized plan designed to teach and reinforce positive behavior. Typically, the plan includes strategies to address behavior that interferes with learning.

Functional performance

Refers to skills or activities that are not related to a child's academic achievement. This term is often used in the context of routine activities of everyday living such as dressing and eating; social skills such as making friends; behavior skills across a range of settings; and mobility skills, such as walking, getting around, and going up and down stairs.

Due process hearing

The legal method a parent can use to formally disagree with the school and make their case for what their child needs. The first step is filing a written complaint related to a child's eligibility for special education services or the types of services he or she receives.

FAPE

Under IDEA, children with disabilities have the right to a free and appropriate public education (FAPE). An education that is "appropriate" is carefully designed to meet a student's individual needs.

Functional Behavioral Assessment (FBA)

An assessment used to uncover why a student is having behavioral issues by identifying the social, emotional and environmental causes. An FBA is typically conducted by a BCBA who will then create a BIP to shape behavior going forward.

General education curriculum

The knowledge and skills that all students throughout a state are expected to master at each grade level.

Goals

The IEP document lists the academic and functional (everyday) skills the IEP team thinks a student can achieve by the end of a school year. These goals are geared toward helping students take part in the general education curriculum.

Individuals with Disabilities Education Act (IDEA)

The federal law governing special education for students with disabilities. IDEA guarantees that qualifying students have access to FAPE within the LRE through the creation of an IEP.

Independent Educational Evaluation (IEE)

An IEE is an evaluation conducted by an expert who is not affiliated with the school. Parents sometimes request an IEE if they disagree with the results of the school's evaluation of their child. The school can request an IEE when they don't have the right experts to evaluate a specific issue or skill set.

Individualized Education Program (IEP)

A written document outlining the program of special education instruction, supports, and services that a student with a disability needs to make progress in school.

Local Education Authority (LEA)

A public school district.

Learning evaluation

Typically conducted during an initial evaluation or reevaluation for special education. Achievement testing focuses on academics—how a student does with school-related skills such as reading, written expression and mathematics, compared to their peers.

Least Restrictive Environment (LRE)

One of the key provisions of IDEA. It means that students with disabilities must be educated in the same setting as peers who don't have disabilities (a general education classroom) to the greatest extent possible.

Manifestation determination

A meeting in which the IEP Team discusses whether or not a child's misbehavior is a symptom, or manifestation, of his or her disability. If so, the student has more protections regarding discipline matters.

Mediation conference

A private meeting where parents and the school try to reach an agreement, with the help of a neutral third party. If successful, a legal agreement will be drafted and signed at the end of the meeting.

Modifications

A change in what a student is expected to learn and demonstrate. For example, a teacher might ask the class to write an essay, while a student with a modification may only be expected to write one paragraph.

Multi-tier System of Support (MTSS)

A structure used by many school districts to provide help for struggling learners in the general education classroom. It is one model for doing Response to Intervention (RTI).

Objectives

The smaller steps (sometimes called benchmarks or short-term objectives) it will take to meet an IEP goal. Often, it's a list of the specific skills necessary to achieve the larger goal.

Present Levels

A description of a student's current abilities, skills, challenges, and strengths at the time the IEP is written. It includes both academic skills (like reading level) and functional skills (like making conversation or writing with a pencil).

Procedural safeguards

A list of the rights that parents and students with disabilities have under the IDEA and its implementing regulations.

Psychological evaluation

Typically conducted during an initial evaluation or reevaluation for special education. Cognitive testing focuses on how a student processes information. An IQ score is obtained to help determine a student's potential for learning.

Parent Training and Information Centers (PTI)

IDEA provides money for each state to have at least one PTI. These centers are designed to help the families of kids from birth to age 26 who have a disability. They offer parents support and free information about special education.

Prior Written Notice (PWN)

Written notice is one of the procedural safeguards for parents under IDEA. It is a formal letter the school sends any time they propose an evaluation or change to special education services, and any time they deny or accept a parent request for the same. It explains what the school plans to do or refuses to do, and the reasoning behind it.

Related services

The support services a student needs to benefit from special education. Some examples include transportation, occupational therapy, speech and language services, counseling, and parent training.

Resolution meeting

A stage of the dispute resolution process that takes place after a parent files a due process complaint. It offers parents and school districts the opportunity to resolve issues prior to a due process hearing.

Response to Intervention (RTI)

A systematic way of identifying struggling students and providing extra help in general education. Teachers assess the skills of everyone in the class to see which students need evidence-based instructional interventions, and then implement them accordingly.

Section 504 of Rehabilitation Act 1973

The first disability civil rights law to be enacted in the U.S. It prohibits discrimination in programs that receive federal funds, such as public schools. A 504 Plan describes the accommodations a school will use to support a student with a disability by removing barriers to learning.

Specially designed instruction

Special education designed to meet the unique needs of a child that result from his or her disability. The plan is outlined in a document called an IEP.

State complaint

If a parent suspects that their school has violated the IDEA, they can file a complaint with their state department of education. After an investigation, a ruling will be made and the school will be expected to take corrective action if necessary.

Stay put

This right comes into play when a parent files for due process because they disagree with a change the school district wants to make in their child's educational placement or services. "Stay put" allows the student to continue to get the same services while the dispute is resolved.

Supplementary aids and services

Supports to enable students with disabilities to learn in both education-related settings, and in nonacademic and extracurricular settings. Examples include equipment such as a wheelchair, assistive technology such as audiobooks, self-management and study skills tools, and participation in social skills groups.

Transition plan

The part of the IEP that lays out a plan for what the student will do after high school. Transition planning starts the year that a student turns 16, and addresses both academic and functional needs. Things like preparation for college, instruction in practical life skills and job training can all be included.

Made in the USA
Las Vegas, NV
10 November 2023

80601136R00128